In Pursuit of Justice

Christian-Democratic Explorations

James W. Skillen

ROWMAN & LITTLEFIELD PUBLISHERS, INC.
Lanham • Boulder • New York • Toronto • Oxford

Published in cooperation with the Center for Public Justice

ROWMAN & LITTLEFIELD PUBLISHERS, INC.

Published in the United States of America
by Rowman & Littlefield Publishers, Inc.
A wholly owned subsidiary of The Rowman & Littlefield Publishing Group, Inc.
4501 Forbes Boulevard, Suite 200, Lanham, Maryland 20706
www.rowmanlittlefield.com

PO Box 317
Oxford
OX2 9RU, UK

Published in cooperation with the Center for Public Justice

British Library Cataloguing in Publication Information Available

Library of Congress Cataloging-in-Publication Data

Skillen, James W.
  In pursuit of justice : Christian-Democratic explorations / James W. Skillen.
    p. cm.
  Includes bibliographical references and index.
  ISBN 0-7425-3523-1 (cloth : alk. paper) — ISBN 0-7425-3524-X (pbk. : alk. paper)
  1. Christianity and politics—United States. 2. Christianity and justice—United States.
3. Christian democracy—United States. I. Title.

  BR526.S585 2004
  261.7—dc22   2004003562

Printed in the United States of America

♾™ The paper used in this publication meets the minimum requirements of American
National Standard for Information Sciences—Permanence of Paper for Printed Library
Materials, ANSI/NISO Z39.48-1992.

Contents

Preface

Democracy now appears to be a self-evident truth throughout most of the world. But what about justice? Is there any agreement, across civilizations, about how to pursue justice? If democracy is the answer to authoritarianism and totalitarianism, will democracy lead to a worldwide agreement about justice?

Christianity is no longer a self-evident truth in the West, though it is growing throughout much of the world. In the minds or experience of many, however, Christianity is associated more with injustice than justice. Yet I will argue that Christianity at its core shines a bright light on both justice and democracy. In fact, the aim of this book is to show why the pursuit of justice in the contemporary world should be a Christian-democratic undertaking.

For too long, the advancement of democracy has been misunderstood as requiring the abandonment or privatization of Christianity and other religions. Religion, however, is not an isolable function that humans can marginalize or emphasize at will. The faiths, including the secular faiths, by which people live direct their lives and not only their modes of worship.

Working critically within the American context, I try in the following chapters to work out some of the implications of a Christian-democratic approach to the meaning of civil society, to welfare and education reform, to racial reconciliation and environmental protection, and to the reform of the electoral system.

Chapter 1 makes a carefully nuanced case for joining the words "Christian" and "democratic" in order to guide the pursuit of justice in complex, pluralistic societies. It briefly explores the rise and decline of Christian-democratic political parties in Europe and assesses the earlier ambiguous connection between Christianity and the republican form of government in America. It introduces basic principles and commitments of a Christian-democratic approach to government and civic responsibility.

In the next chapter, contemporary expressions of interest in civil society bring into focus questions about government's relation to the wide array of nongovernment institutions and organizations of society. Democracy in itself sheds no light on how the political community should both support and remain distinguished from that which is nongovernmental. Herein lies a fundamental question of justice.

The third chapter takes us to the root of the supposedly self-evident truth of democracy. What does it mean to be human? In what sense are humans self-governing? Since humans are complex, multifaceted, social creatures, there is more to human life than political governance. How should democracy serve men, women, and children in the deepest, broadest meaning of their lives?

Chapter 4 takes up justice in welfare policy, particularly as it concerns the relation of government to a diverse range of nonprofit organizations actively serving those in need. Most social service organizations are religious. Thus, the question arises, how can a democratic government do justice to the poor if it does not give equal treatment to all social service organizations—including religious organizations—when government cooperates with them to serve the poor? The answer from a Christian-democratic perspective is that justice requires genuine pluralism and equal treatment of all.

Racial justice demands the end of legalized discrimination against African Americans and other minorities. Yet African Americans are more than merely black people. They are complex, multifaceted, social creatures like everyone else. A Christian-democratic perspective helps illumine the requirement of racial nondiscrimination in an all-inclusive political community where justice can be done to citizens only by doing justice to human beings who are always more than citizens.

Chapter 6 proposes a radical reform of the public governance of education based on the principles of justice and pluralism articulated in preceding chapters. The political community must be all-inclusive and nondiscriminatory, but it can be such a community only by protecting the rights and responsibilities of diverse families and schools.

The seventh chapter presents a stark contrast between the highly problematic, interest-group approach to environmental protection offered by the liberal-democratic tradition, and a Christian-democratic approach that points the way to justice for the commons. Here we expose John Locke's fundamental misinterpretation of the creation story.

Finally, at the heart of democracy is the voice of the people, usually incorporated into government by a system of elections through which the people gain representation in legislative and executive offices and hold public officials accountable. From a Christian-democratic point of view it is all too apparent, however, that the American electoral system is not democratic enough. Chapter 8 makes the case for a major reform of the American electoral system, a reform that is necessary if justice is to be done to the citizens of this democracy.

Acknowledgments

This book could not have been written without the encouragement of my colleagues at the Center for Public Justice, particularly Stanley Carlson-Thies, Stephen Lazarus, and Jack Boeve, and the Center's trustees and many supporters. Nor could it have been written without Doreen's enduring support. I also want to thank the Earhart Foundation for a grant that encouraged the research and writing of some parts of the book. Earlier versions of a number of the chapters were written for journals and other book projects. Thus, a sincere expression of thanks is in order for permission to use and revise that material.

An earlier version of chapter 2 appeared in the book *Local Ownership, Global Change*, edited by Roland Hoksbergen and Lowell Ewert, copyright © 2002, and is used by permission of World Vision International. An earlier version of chapter 3 appeared as "The Question of Being Human in Assessing the Requirements of Welfare Policy Reform" in *Welfare in America: Christian Perspectives on a Policy in Crisis*, edited by Stanley W. Carlson-Thies and James W. Skillen, copyright © 1996 Wm. B. Eerdmans Publishing Co., Grand Rapids, Michigan. Used by permission. An earlier version of chapter 4 first appeared in *The Princeton Seminary Bulletin* 22, no. 2 (2001): 285–305, and is used with permission. Much of the material from a chapter in *Religion, Race, and Justice in a Changing America* (1999), edited by Gary Orfield and Holly J. Lebowitz, was used in chapter 5 by permission of the Century Foundation. An earlier version of chapter 6 was published in *The Journal of Law and Politics* 6, no. 3 (Spring 1990) and is used by the journal's permission. Chapter 8 is an expansion and revision of a chapter in my book *Recharging the American Experiment* (Baker Books, a division of Baker Book House Company, 1994).

James W. Skillen
Annapolis, Maryland

CHAPTER ONE

⌐

What Distinguishes a Christian-Democratic Point of View?

Joining the words "Christian" and "Democracy" undoubtedly raises questions. The combination suggests a compatibility, but what does the word "Christian" add? Isn't democracy simply democracy, and by its nature isn't a democratic society open to everyone without religious qualification? A democracy is a community of citizens, not a community of faith. There is nothing peculiarly Christian about it. The word combination is, thus, superfluous, is it not?

Considered from another point of view, perhaps there is something incompatible between the two elements of the hyphenated adjective. Didn't the rise of democratic governments in the West generally undermine the establishment of Christianity? If so, doesn't the use of the word "Christian" in connection with contemporary democracy suggest that Christians still have designs to control government even if they are now willing to work through democratic means to try to gain that control? In that case, the combination is fraught with ambiguity and perhaps even a dangerous tension.

A third possibility, suggested by Robert Kraynak, is that Christians have been willing to relinquish too much of what is distinctively Christian in their rush to become supporters of democracy. Most Christians today, Kraynak writes, "believe that the form of government most compatible with the Christian religion is democracy."[1] But that is not a particularly good sign for Christianity, according to Kraynak. Christians have accommodated themselves too much to the all-embracing secular state, accepting the disestablishment of the church and, to varying degrees, the privatization of

1

Christianity. This is a problem both for Christianity and for sound government, because in Kraynak's view secular democracy and Christianity are not fully compatible. The word "Christian," when combined with "democracy," may thus serve as a weak adjective representing a self-inflicted wound.

There is, however, another interpretation of the combination, and it provides the underlying thesis for the explorations of this book. Two important distinctions are necessary at the outset. First, there is a difference between using the word "Christian" or "Christianity" to refer to a normative pattern or normative standards for life, on the one hand, and using the word to refer to actual churches and communities of people throughout history who have identified themselves as Christians, on the other hand. Christians, in practice, do not necessarily conform to Christian normative standards; rather, those standards often call their practices into question. Second, there is a difference between referring to democracy as a system of representative government open equally to all citizens, and using the word "democracy" in an ideological way to insist that all authority and principles for government reside in, and arise from, autonomous individuals or "the people."

I want to argue that human responsibility before God in conformity with God's creating, judging, and redeeming work in Jesus Christ is not only compatible with democracy as a system of representative government, but actually calls for it. In other words, the truth of God's creation, human sin, and God's redeeming judgment, when properly understood, lays the foundation for an open society whose just governance requires the equal treatment of all citizens without regard to their faith, and calls for the accountability of government to them. At the same time, Christianity as normative pattern for life is quite incompatible with the ideology of democratism, because, from a Christian point of view, the normative standards for the just governance of a community of citizens derive ultimately from the Creator, not from the people. By the same token, what we generally identify as the "Christian" societies of the medieval and early modern period do not represent *the* normative pattern of just governance, but rather display the accommodation of Christians to patterns and ideals of Roman imperialism and its attendant influences and consequences.

My thesis can now be summarized as follows: a Christian-democratic approach to government represents a positive advance, a move away from past accommodations to imperialist and statist structures and ideologies toward a more normative Christian realization of public justice. But a Christian-democratic approach will exist in tension and sometimes in conflict with approaches grounded in an ideological commitment to democracy—

democratism—as it will with other political ideologies, even as it insists on equal political treatment of every citizen without regard to their ideological commitment or faith.

Before elaborating on this thesis in the next two sections, a few additional clarifications are necessary. First, the tension between what Christians are called to do and what they actually do remains a problem. Therefore, Christians should never claim that their achievements or their aims in politics or in any other arena of life represent God's will. They should claim only that they are trying to respond obediently to God's call to love their neighbors and to do justice. That way they remain open to correction and reproof from fellow Christians and from all their civic neighbors. Admittedly, the words "Christian-democratic" can be problematic, because the word "Christian" may suggest an identification of the fallible political efforts of Christians with God's will. Instead, the words should be used to convey the modest aim or aspiration of those who are trying to contribute to a justly governed, democratically open society.

Second, a Christian-democratic approach to politics and government *does* represent an attempt to bring a distinctive point of view into political debates and the work of government. Even this is something that many Christians and non-Christians alike find unacceptable, particularly if they think of Christianity as a private matter or identify it with an impositional approach to politics that is incompatible with democracy. Nevertheless, if normative Christianity represents God's call to faithful service in all arenas of life, then trying to develop a Christian approach to politics is as necessary and legitimate as the attempt by liberals and conservatives, libertarians and socialists, to develop an approach to politics consistent with their deepest commitments.

Of course, many Christians may consider themselves conservative or socialist or libertarian, politically speaking, and will not be sympathetic to a Christian-democratic approach. That is precisely what an open, democratic political system should allow. The aim of a Christian-democratic approach to politics is not to try to divide Christians along political lines, or to separate Christian citizens from non-Christian citizens, or to claim divine favor for its political agenda. Instead, the aim is to bring into public debate a point of view not offered by those of other political persuasions and ideologies. This is why citizens oriented by a Christian-democratic perspective should, as a matter of principle, work for an electoral system that makes room for all groups of citizens to contend with one another freely and openly in political debate from out of their distinctive points of view.

Before elaborating on some of the essential ingredients of a Christian-democratic perspective, we must first situate ourselves historically.

Historical Touch Points

No political party or movement in the United States has laid claim to a Christian-democratic name or identity. The situation in Europe, Latin America, and a few other places in the world has been different, however.[2] Does this perhaps suggest that the very idea of a Christian-democratic approach to politics makes no sense in the United States?

From one perspective, the history of modern politics in the West has been the struggle to overcome Christian imperialism and intolerance.[3] The Reformation and early state building in Europe challenged the claims of the Holy Roman Empire from within Christendom itself. Then, as sovereign states took shape, the question of inclusiveness and exclusiveness—of tolerance and intolerance—in defining citizenship grew in importance. Could a unified state be maintained without a common faith or an established church, and if so, how? If Christian faith should no longer be a qualification for full citizenship, then what glue would hold the political order together? Most westerners believe these questions were answered in the two centuries between the American Revolution and Vatican II in the early 1960s by means of the triumph of enlightened, secular reason. The Enlightenment supposedly won out over intolerant Christianity, or as Jeffrey Rosen describes it, over "religion's wilder, more mystical and irrational aspects."[4]

The American experiment does not fit unambiguously into this interpretation of early modern history, however. It is true that the United States was the first western country to disestablish the church and to set out on a so-called secular political course. On the other hand, the dominant ideology at the time of the American founding was not secular democratism. It was a unique blend that Mark Noll identifies as "Christian republicanism,"[5] which privileged cultural Protestantism in a general way while building a political system that was actually designed to protect government from the threat of mob democracy. From a contemporary Christian-democratic perspective with global resonance, many aspects of the early American republic were clearly unjust, including its slave system and the fact that voting rights belonged only to male property owners. At the same time, some of the major components of just government, recognized throughout much of the world today and certainly by Christian-democratic proponents, first took shape in the American colonial era, or at the founding in 1776–1789, or in the early decades of U.S. history, though some of those components derived from earlier British and Dutch experience. The components of which I am speaking include, for example, a written constitution that defines and qualifies the responsibilities of government under the rule of law; representation of citizens in government by means of regular, fair, and competitive elections; religious freedom and other basic rights for individuals; judicial and administrative processes that are transparent and open to reform; and civilian control of the military.

In the early history of the United States, these and other elements of constitutional democracy were seen as both Christian and enlightened. Many Americans considered the United States to be God's uniquely chosen Christian republic, a city set on a hill as a model for all the world. Others, like Thomas Jefferson, were inclined more toward Enlightenment convictions and considered the United States to be the first new nation that had the potential to become a republic of reason—a republic that would consign dogmatic religion to private quarters. By the time of the Civil War, which represented the breakdown of the original republic, an American civil religion was emerging that blended elements of Christianity, republicanism, liberalism, populism, and nationalism. No major movement of American citizens arose to try to articulate a Christian-democratic perspective on government in contrast to other ideological perspectives such as liberalism, democratism, and republicanism. Rather, Americans fashioned political parties with pragmatic regional and economic interests in mind, all of which took for granted the Protestant Christian identity of the country. The United States didn't seem to need a distinctively Christian political voice. Even the great divide over slavery and the Civil War found both sides defending themselves on a Christian basis with appeals to the Bible.[6]

By contrast, the French Revolution forced many European Christians to confront a deliberate and sharp anti-Christian assault.[7] Some Catholics and Protestants became reactionaries, hoping that the older, prerevolutionary order could be recovered. Others became secular liberals or socialists in the course of the nineteenth century as they left Christianity behind or tried to confine it to private quarters outside the political realm. However, many Christians looked for another path into the future that was neither reactionary nor secularistic. They are the ones who did the spade work for the Christian-democratic political movements that would emerge in Europe and in Latin America beginning late in the nineteenth and early in the twentieth centuries.[8]

Sadly, through a gradual secularization process that has picked up steam in the last few decades, most Christian-democratic parties of Europe and Latin America have lost much of their identity as "parties of Christian inspiration." So it is not as if we can point today to a host of vibrant political movements around the world that march under a Christian-democratic banner. Nonetheless, if we take into account some of the elements that were important in the founding of the United States and in the development of some of the Christian-democratic movements in nineteenth- and twentieth-century Europe, and now in many parts of the world, we can identify many ingredients of the kind of Christian-democratic approach we will explore in this book.

Of first importance here is not so much the question of political party formation, but rather the clarification of differences among ideological commitments that are competing today to shape and control nations around the world. Christian-democratic efforts in Europe arose largely as a counter to atheistic and anti-Christian movements carried along by secularistic ideologies. Catholics and Protestants held views of the person, family life, education, the church, and society that were different from the views of liberal individualists and socialist collectivists. Many such Christians were willing to give up established churches and aristocratic patterns of social and economic life, but they refused to give up their Christian faith or to confine it to worship and prayer, leaving behind an appeal to Christianity's normative standards for all of life. The question was whether Christians had anything distinctive to say about the political, social, and economic changes unfolding so rapidly around them, particularly changes associated with the growing impact of science, the Industrial Revolution, European empire-building, and the crises brought on by two World Wars and the Great Depression.

In the United States, by contrast, Christianity was never directly threatened by attacks from atheistic liberal and socialist political movements. American Christians themselves are the ones who gradually accepted the privatization of the "sectarian" elements of Christianity even as they transferred the idea of God's specially chosen people from the church to the nation, adopting a great deal of liberal-republican political ideology as they went along. Then, between the Civil War and World War II, when the United States grew from an emerging power to dominant global superpower, a gradually secularizing pragmatism took over as the driving force of politics and economic life, amalgamating nationalist, civil-religious, liberal, and Christian convictions into a public ethos of American exceptionalism, which was validated, in the judgment of its adherents, by the success of American leadership in promoting economic growth and democracy at home and abroad.

After World War II, the further secularization of American schools, the media, the law, and the broader culture eventually reached a point, however, where publicly significant protests and reexaminations set in, driving many Americans to search anew for the sure foundations, or at least the secure future, of their democratic republic. Beginning with the civil rights movement and protests over the Vietnam War and continuing through to the current turmoil over terrorism and the worldwide revitalization of religions, the "American way of life" and America's role in the world have come under ever closer scrutiny and criticism. The Enlightenment-liberal faith in straightforward historical progress from religious oppression to rational freedom and democracy is now acknowledged by more and more people to be a myth, though a myth that still controls much of American political rhetoric. The question is whether there are any alternative myths or philosophies— ancient or modern—by which to act in the political world today? What do Americans want? What do they believe? In the past two decades, hundreds of books have rolled off the presses from authors in search of the foundations of democracy and the origin of modern ideologies, seeking explanations for the crisis of Enlightenment faith and the continuing vitality of diverse religions, and rethinking the political meaning of Christianity.[9] This is the context in which the pursuit of justice from a Christian-democratic perspective must find its way.

Ingredients of a Christian-Democratic Perspective

What can a Christian-democratic approach contribute to current inquiries and debates? Is it possible that Christians throughout the world, including the United States, living in vastly different political, economic, and cultural conditions, might be able to do more in the opening decades of the twenty-first century to encourage one another in making distinctive contributions to the democratic governance of the societies in which they live? A more expansive historical and philosophical justification for the arguments developed in the following chapters must await another volume. Yet I believe the essays here—drawn largely from American experience—can illustrate the fruitfulness of a Christian-democratic approach to major constitutional and policy issues today. To conclude this introductory chapter, then, let us consider some of the key ingredients of a Christian-democratic point of view.

Differentiating State and Society

The first important element of a Christian-democratic perspective arises from the nature of human responsibility in God's world. Human responsibility is diversified, requiring different kinds of effort and various types of organization for its achievement. To think only of a family, a business enterprise, a school, a hospital, and a political party is to be aware immediately of very different kinds of human activity, manifesting diverse skills, degrees of cooperation, modes of reasoning and planning, and types of service. All of these express something of what it means to be human—to be a creature created in the image of God. Historically, these various kinds of responsibility have differentiated into identifiable vocations, institutions, and organizations. Nothing is sacrosanct (and much is faulty) about the way any of these is organized in the United States or Brazil or China today, but each (and, of course, many others beside) calls for attention and development if human beings are to experience the richness of what it means to be human.

At the same time, none of these types of responsibility provides the common denominator, the all-inclusive purpose, of all the others. In order to speak of human life and community as a *whole* it is necessary, from a Christian point of view, to refer the entire complex of responsibilities to its source in the Creator, the one for whom all things have been created. This means that no human institution—whether nation, church, state, or empire—can serve as the omnicompetent authority and controlling center for all of human life. The fundamental bias of a Christian-democratic perspective is that every type of imperial hierarchy, every kind of statism, every kind of authoritarianism and totalitarianism, whether oriented by a nationalistic, economic, or security aim, violates human life in community. Consequently, as the great variety of human responsibilities become differentiated historically, it is crucial that the public-legal order—the political community under government—should become differentiated as well.

The political community—the state—is, by its very nature, a public-legal community that organizes everyone in a particular territory under its law. The state is, in this sense, an all-embracing community in contrast to other kinds of organizations and institutions. Yet, from a Christian-democratic perspective, this is precisely why the state needs to be clearly defined and constitutionally limited to its distinctive purpose of establishing and upholding public justice for everyone in the territory of its jurisdiction. The all-embracing legal responsibility of the state can be fulfilled justly only by doing justice to the full meaning of human life, including all of the nongovernment or nonstate institutions and responsibilities. The political community embraces families, banks, business enterprises, schools, and hospitals, but only for the purpose of binding them together in a public-legal way to realize a healthy political community for all. The political community has no authority to act directly in the place of parents, bank trustees, business owners, teachers, and doctors.

This argument for limited government is quite different from the argument offered by classical liberalism—the ideology from which Americans derive both conservative and liberal versions. Government should be limited, say Christian-democratic proponents, not because individuals are the original sovereigns over themselves, but rather because governments have a particular, differentiated, calling to uphold a community of public justice. This leads to another contrast with classical liberalism. A Christian-democratic perspective affirms the importance of the political community—the federal republic, in the American case—as one of the important expressions of human identity and meaning. This is the conviction that humans were created for political community as well as for family life, economic life, and everything else. From a liberal perspective, political community is not natural for free individuals. Rather, humans should be as individually free and autonomous as possible. Submitting to government may be necessary if one wants the protection of one's life and property, but it is not a part of our original identity, according to liberal ideology. From a Christian-democratic perspective, by contrast, the healthy differentiation of society is only possible if a political community also emerges to become the public-legal guardian of the commons in which the great variety of differentiated responsibilities can all develop and flourish simultaneously.

The Dignity of the Person

Catholic social thought in particular has emphasized the "dignity of the person" as a way of capturing the idea that humans have an identity and destiny that transcends the purpose and authority of the state. Or to express it in positive political terms, governments have an obligation to protect human rights, including religious freedom and most fundamentally human life at all stages, in order to do justice to the full meaning of the person. This is the basis on which the Catholic Church now defends democracy.

> The Church recognizes that while democracy is the best expression of the direct participation of citizens in political choices, it succeeds only to the extent that it is based on a correct understanding of the human *person*. Catholic involvement in political life cannot compromise on this principle, for otherwise the witness of the Christian faith in the world, as well as the unity and interior coherence of the faithful, would be nonexistent. The democratic structures on which the modern state is based would be quite fragile were its foundations not the centrality of the human person. It is respect for the person that makes democratic participation possible.[10]

Since humans have been made for life in community and for service to God, this is another way of arguing that state and society must become differentiated in order to make possible the development of all the talents and responsibilities of persons who are ultimately responsible to God, not to the state or to other institutions.

An important moment of truth in liberalism, in this regard, is its recognition that the mature adult should be recognized as a responsible person and not reduced to a mere pawn of the state or to some other role or relationship. This insight was made possible by the development of open societies in connection with the historical differentiation of the modern political community. In other words, the development of a public-legal order, in which the independence of other associations and institutions are recognized, has also opened up a sphere of private civil law in which people are recognized as free persons—as individuals—and not only as family members, employees, students, spouses, church members, and citizens. A just state or political community not only recognizes the independent authorities and responsibilities of nongovernment organizations and institutions. It also recognizes and protects the rights of individual persons as such.

There was a time when a woman was recognized in law only as the spouse or daughter of a man. She could not, on her own, enter into a business contract or vote. There was a time when a peasant had no independent identity apart from his relation to the feudal lord's property and political authority. There was a time when an individual had rights only if he or she belonged to the right family, or was a member of the established church, or owned property. The differentiation of the state as a public-legal community distinct from family privilege, race, ecclesiastical authority, aristocratic privilege, and economic position has made it possible not only for different social institutions and relationships to come into their own, but also for individuals to be recognized as having civil rights and individual freedoms. This is, of course, another reason why an overreaching government or totalitarian state is unjust, because it acts wholly or in part as the controlling authority over individual lives, refusing to recognize the full dignity of persons both in their individual identity and in their responsibilities in nonpolitical institutions and relationships.

The error of liberal ideology is to take the moment of truth about individual freedom under the law and to absolutize it as the origin and source of authority for all human relationships and obligations, including the state. The dignity of the person, from this perspective, resides in his or her individual autonomy. The fact that under the law of a just state an individual is free to enter into contracts and other relationships suggests to the liberal that the individual is self-authorizing and self-governing from the start, prior to all social obligations and responsibilities, prior even to the state. From that starting point, the classical liberal then imagines that every human relationship and institution is created by individuals as a reflex of their own interests and autonomy.

From a Christian-democratic perspective, however, liberal ideology has mistakenly absolutized the truth of *relative* individual freedom, which can come to expression only with the emergence of a differentiated state and society. The only way to do justice simultaneously to (1) individual freedom, (2) multiple spheres of social responsibility, and (3) civic responsibility in the political community is to start with the recognition of human beings as created in the image of God for many different kinds of responsibility, none of which supplies the reductionistic purpose or center for the whole of human life.[11] If socialists err by trying to reduce persons to their role or function in the economy or the state, then liberals err by trying to reduce the full panoply of social life to individual freedom. Both reductionisms fail, because human persons, created in the image of God, are neither autonomous individuals nor mere extensions of families, clans, nations, corporations, or states.

This is why religious freedom has to be a fundamental civil right, from a Christian-democratic point of view. Since humans have their dignity because they have been created in the image of God, their ultimate obligation is to God, not to a state or an enterprise or a clan. Or to put it in another way, even in and through their civic responsibility, humans owe that responsibility ultimately to God. There is no human institution that can stand in the place of God and call for the ultimate allegiance of individuals and all of society to itself. Through churches and similar institutions people express their communal allegiance to God in worship and service. Not only must such institutions be free of state control, but individuals and all nongovernment institutions and organizations must be free of internal state control in order to be able to exercise their responsibility in those spheres to God. The political community exists to uphold public justice for all, and that must include doing justice to persons who owe their ultimate obligation to God, even if many citizens decide to serve idols or to deny that they owe any obligation to God. Those decisions have to be an expression of their own responsibility, not something compelled by the government.

In this regard, the long history of imperial and religiously discriminatory governments reveals a political and legal error. The Christian-democratic argument is that since Christians have been called to bear witness to the God whose rain and sunshine fall on the just and unjust alike and to bear witness that none but God has authority to separate the wheat and the tares in the field of the divine kingdom, then on that basis alone there is every reason to renounce the mistaken identification of a political community with a community of Christian faith. In fact, Christianity, uncoupled from the imperial pattern, has its own biblical grounds for advocating government's equal treatment of all citizens, regardless of their faith. All people have been created in

God's image and given responsibility in God's one world, which, according to the New Testament, is being judged and redeemed through Jesus Christ. From this point of view, equal justice for all finds its firmest basis in the creation-sustaining grace of the Creator-Redeemer, not in human reason, altruism, autonomy, or interest-group power balances. Moreover, the grace of God grants to Christians no political privileges or right to conquer others.

However, as soon as we grant that a political community need not and should not be qualified as a community of faith, we have to clarify the terms of the distinction between those two types of community. The distinction cannot be one of simple, mutual exclusiveness, as if faith and religion belong in one watertight box and politics and citizenship in another. Christians (and people of some other faiths) confess that God lays total claim to their lives, including their political lives. Moreover, Christians in this world are not merely *citizens* who happen to live by faith; they are also children and parents, friends and scholars, engineers and business people, artists and farmers, who live, or ought to live, by the same faith in God in all spheres of life.

The political community cannot be separated or isolated from the religions of its citizens. A political community encompasses everyone within its territory as citizens or subjects, but citizens are people who can never be reduced to their civic identity alone. *People* are always more than *citizens*. The real question then about the distinction between a community of faith and a political community concerns the unique qualification or principle of inclusion for each community and how the two ought to be related.

In posing the question this way, we can see immediately that the typical dichotomy of "religion and politics" used almost universally by the media and by most westerners is simply misleading. Religion, in the standard formula, is usually thought of as an isolable function or institutional affiliation quite separate from politics, business, sports, and the weather. Such a formula may fit comfortably with a religiously deep Enlightenment worldview, namely one that considers all of reality to be subject to the sovereignty of enlightened reason, a sovereign that has authority to confine religion to private quarters. But this dichotomy does not belong to a Christian view of reality. Christians testify to the God who is not only very public, but who claims all authority in heaven and on earth. The Christian way of life is not a private cult, a gnostic mystery, or a personal preference. It cannot be confined to private quarters.[12] The God of heaven and earth cannot be kept out of politics.

From a Christian-democratic perspective, this insistent, public, Christian faith requires, on its own terms, the rejection of every monopolistic, imperial claim to control of the political order by anyone or any institution, including the church and those who profess faith in Christ. To do justice to the dignity of the person, a Christian-democratic approach insists on rejecting a privatized understanding of religion *as well as* any discriminatory political imperialism carried out in the name of Christ. On the basis of the Christian confession itself, advocates of Christian-democracy call for equal treatment of all citizens regardless of their confessional orientation and affiliation. Christianity, in other words, is a public and not merely a private religion, and its principled public advocacy—grounded in God's authority not in human sovereignty—should aim for equal justice for all. Christian grounds for an open and religiously nondiscriminatory state, qualified as a community of citizens rather than as a community of faith, lie deeper than the terms for tolerating religion offered by either Enlightenment reason or modern pragmatism. From a Christian-democratic perspective, the dignity of the very image of God is at stake.

Economic Justice

The question of economic justice in a differentiated society must be addressed from at least two different angles. The first concerns the just treatment of economically productive activity and market exchanges as they are organized through firms and corporations, bringing together workers, managers, investors, buyers, and sellers. The second concerns the just ordering of society for the economic good of all, including the good of families, schools, nonprofit organizations, and the political community. The tendency of liberalism moving in the direction of libertarianism is to say that if life, property, and free markets are protected, most other goods will take care of themselves as a consequence of economic progress. The tendency of liberalism moving in the direction of socialism is to say that if social solidarity is protected by means of public policies that assure greater economic equality, then economic productivity and exchanges will take care of themselves. Approaching the question of economic justice from a Christian-democratic point of view means something quite different.

Economic productivity and market exchanges entail a diversity of human capabilities and responsibilities, ranging from different kinds of agriculture to a host of technologies, from commerce in thousands of products to many types of heavy industry. The law and government must do justice to all of these, none of which exists solely to "make a profit," though without profit making, few if any of them could continue to function. At the same time, the human beings engaged in all of these activities are always more than producers and consumers in a marketplace. They are citizens in a shared political community; they are parents and children, teachers and students, neighbors and friends, members of churches and voluntary associations. Justice must be done to all of these relationships, organizations, and institutions simultaneously in order for human life to flourish. The purpose of the political community—the state—is precisely to constitute and uphold a community of public justice for all.

As we will consider in chapters 2 and 7, in particular, a fundamental condition of economic justice is a justly ordered political community and just international law. It is the constitutional responsibility of a representative government to uphold the well-being of the commons—the public square—including the rules of the market in which economic productivity and exchange take place. Control of weights and measures; printing money and controlling the money supply; determining the legal definition of the corporation; establishing labor laws, transportation laws, laws of contract and tort, and anti-monopoly laws—these and many more make a market possible. The market, in this sense, is part of the public square, the commons, the public-legal order. It is the responsibility of government, with democratically represented citizens, to make these public-legal decisions. Without public laws and regulations, there would be no free market: no limit to the use of children in sweat shops, no restrictions on slave labor, no inhibition of monopolies, no fines for counterfeit money, no penalties for the sale of dangerous goods through false advertising.

The fact that a free market depends on all of these public-legal conditions is usually presented as a seeming paradox or a problem from a free-market point of view. Robert Nelson summarizes "the problem" this way:

> The market is based on the idea of individual pursuit of self-interest. At the same time, however, a market system will work best if there is a clear limit to self-interest. The pursuit of self-interest should not extend to various forms of opportunism, such as cheating, lying, and other types of deception, misrepresentation, and corruption within the marketplace. Self-interest should not extend to "political opportunism," the attempt to use government to coercively extract benefits from others or to protect each business firm and each worker from any negative consequences in the normal workings of market competition (say, by demanding a tariff to protect against job losses from international trade). Another key consideration is that property rights, contracts, and other legal arrangements should be fairly and consistently enforced. In short, the market must exist within an institutional and civic-value context that transcends individual self-interest and supports and encourages actions that have a wider benefit for the common good.[13]

For this reason, says Nelson, "the development of a satisfactory constitutional framework and its enforcement . . . may be critical to the effective functioning of a market system. Yet this may be a difficult requirement to meet. In some ways it depends on simultaneously encouraging and discouraging the expression of self-interest" (269).

There is no difficulty or paradox here, however, if one recognizes that the full human self-in-community has many "interests" and responsibilities from the start, not just an economic self-interest. And not all expressions of self-interest are acts of selfishness. Human beings have a legitimate self-interest in healthy families and friendships, in clean air and water, in opportunities to worship God and to serve neighbors in need, in working and developing their talents, in reading and writing and listening to music. These interests are not somehow thwarted or dampened by either a conscience that keeps individuals from lying and cheating or a public-legal order that defines and backs up rules of the market. To the contrary, the realization of genuine self-interest requires just such a normative context.

Economic justice, from a Christian-democratic point of view, does not mean calling on government to counter every self-interested decision by business people, laborers, and consumers in order to achieve a more moral (and less self-interested society). Government has no more of a right or responsibility to stand in the place of business and labor than it does to stand in the place of parents, teachers, and ecclesiastical authorities. At the same time, however, it is precisely government's responsibility to establish and uphold laws for the good of all citizens in the political community, including all the institutions and organizations they initiate and in which they participate. This responsibility will indeed require government's action at times to curb actions by people that endanger public justice or threaten the lives of citizens and the well-being of the political community. Human beings have a legitimate interest in, and a responsibility for, a peaceful and healthy political community at the same time that they have an interest in and responsibility for families, other human relationships, and strictly qualified economic activity.

What is missing or very weak in American public life, however, is a commitment to the political community as a valuable part of human identity and proper self-interest in this world. Consequently, we Americans tend to pit government and the free market against one another. This is largely the consequence of our commitment to one version or another of liberal ideology, with the consequences to be discussed in chapters 7 and 8. Individual freedom supposedly comes first; government comes second only as a grudging necessity to protect our lives and freedoms. Government thought of in these terms means that it stands over against us as "them"—as a perpetual threat to our freedom with its rules and taxes. Only if this mistaken liberal view of human nature, society, markets, and government is replaced by a view of human life that includes political community as part of our true identity as God's image will it be possible to develop a healthy, pluralistic society that makes full room for a free and open economic marketplace in the context of a just political community and just international order.

International Justice
Although this book does not take up a consideration of international politics and foreign policy, we must emphasize that government, from a Christian-democratic point of view, necessarily entails an international perspective and responsibility. Human responsibility in this world should be exercised with full awareness that this is God's *one* world and that humans everywhere share the same identity as the image of God. There are both good and bad reasons for the widespread division of governing responsibility among human communities throughout the world. The dominant form of political community today is the modern state. Yet states do not live in isolated separation from one another. With each passing year, the interdependence of peoples and states increases. Partly as a result of two world wars and the Cold War, many important international organizations have been created to help facilitate the governance of the international commons. These include defense organizations like NATO (the North Atlantic Treaty Organization), economic organizations like the WTO (the World Trade Organization), and multifunctional organizations like the United Nations (UN).

While it is true that the governments of different states have as their primary responsibility to govern the people within their own territories, it is illegitimate to define that responsibility solely in nationalist or statist terms. There is too much about the global commons that calls for cooperation among states to achieve international justice. Dangers such as international terrorism, environmental degradation, and the maldistribution of the earth's resources require international efforts to thwart them. Positive advantages such as trade, cross-cultural exchanges and understanding, and the peaceful settlement of disputes require international cooperation to promote them. A Christian-democratic approach emphasizes a commitment to international justice and the exercise of national governance in ways that help to strengthen responsible, accountable, international organizations. This has nothing to do with a dreamy idealism about global peace, particularly if the reality with which we are dealing includes highly unjust states whose governments are not accountable to their citizens. International justice cannot be built on domestic injustice and disorder. State building of a solid, constitutional, accountable kind is as necessary as the development of international law organizations. In fact, both processes have to unfold at the same time.

From a Christian-democratic point of view, the normative concern is with just governance, not first of all with a particular form of political organization. The governance of political communities, of whatever kind, will increasingly be exercised in a globe of ever more interdependent peoples, states, and a vast array of nongovernment institutions and organizations. The demands of justice in such a world cannot be met by competing nationalisms, state or regional empire building, or dreamy talk of global peace. The pursuit of justice must be dogged and determined both domestically and internationally, and those who share a Christian-democratic point of view will have to demonstrate the value and integrity of their commitment by cooperating together both within their own states and across all state boundaries for the good of their neighbors everywhere.

CHAPTER TWO

≈

Civil Society and
Human Development

What Constitutes Civil Society?

In one of many recent books on "civil society" in the United States—
Community Works: The Revival of Civil Society in America[1]—the editor,
E. J. Dionne Jr., writes,

> The definition that runs through this book is straightforward, summarized
> well by Benjamin Barber in his book, *A Place for Us*. Civil Society is "an in-
> dependent domain of free social life where neither governments nor private
> markets are sovereign." It is "a realm we create for ourselves through associ-
> ated common action in families, clans, churches and communities." It is a
> "third sector" that "mediates between our specific individuality as economic
> producers and consumers and our abstract collectivity as members of a sover-
> eign people" (2–3).

Brian O'Connell, the author of *Civil Society: The Underpinnings of American
Democracy*,[2] whose stated purpose is to clarify the meaning of "civil society,"
says that "the most common agreement about civil society is that it represents the balance between the rights granted to individuals in free societies
and the responsibilities required of citizens to maintain those rights"
(11–12). Further on, O'Connell writes, "Civil society exists at the intersection where the various elements of society come together to protect and nurture the individual and where the individual operates to provide those same
protections and liberating opportunities for others" (24).

Notice the vagueness, ambiguities, and multiple meanings emanating from just these two representative books. "Civil society" refers both to a "domain" (or "realm") as well as to institutions, such as families, clans, and churches. The phrase is used as a singular noun, yet a noun that refers to almost every conceivable kind of organization, relationship, or associated common action that can be distinguished from government and the organizations of economic production and consumption. However, even that is to say too little, for O'Connell contends that government is the "third component of civil society" (18) along with the individual and community. The difficulty in nailing down the meaning of "civil society" only intensifies if we take into consideration its contemporary usage in Eastern Europe and parts of the Third World and if we entertain the views of a diverse range of theorists, including John Locke, G. W. F. Hegel, Alexis de Tocqueville, and Vaclav Havel.

Because of this ambiguity, which is due to the wide variety of descriptive and normative uses of the term, I will place "civil society" in quotation marks throughout this chapter. My aim in doing so is not to marginalize or belittle the phrase, but rather to help make room for the development of a normative view of human society that can overcome many of the ambiguities and confusions inherent in its current uses.[3] In particular, my concern is to explore the meaning of both the "domain" and the "organizations" of "civil society." The argument to be developed in this chapter can be summarized in a few paragraphs:

The kind of historical unfolding or differentiation of human institutions and associations that we have experienced in the West has led inevitably to the need for an ever sharper identification of the distinguishable identities and responsibilities of those institutions and associations. This differentiation process has also created the need for answers to questions about how the diverse types of organizations ought to be properly interrelated. The historical process of social differentiation and integration is evident now throughout the world, albeit in different ways, yet almost always influenced by western-led globalization. There are, for example, the ongoing domestic and international public-legal struggles to distinguish the responsibilities of governments and of business corporations in relation to one another and in relation to all the other responsibilities and relationships people have.

The "space," or "domain," or "intersection" of all the different institutions and relationships, I will argue, is one and the same for all of them, though it is variously referred to as the "public square," the "commons," or the "open space of free societies." This "space" is made possible by law-making and law-enforcing governments, whose responsibilities, normatively stated, are precisely to do justice to all—to everything and everyone within their territories at the same time and in the same public space. In this respect, what is usually referred to as the "market" (both domestic and international) is part of the public domain as defined by rules that govern economic life: the rules of trade and commerce, of weights and measures, of incorporation and taxation, and so forth. But in that same public "commons" there are also many nongovernmental and non-economic organizations and relationships that must be distinguished, identified, and protected in public law in order to be able to fulfill their own responsibilities. Each nongovernmental and non-economic organization has its own identity and purpose—family, friendship, university, hospital, church, sports club, political interest group, community organization, and hundreds more.

Part of the ambiguity in the use of the phrase "civil society" arises because of a desire to group everything that is *neither* "economic" *nor* "governmental" into a single category for easy reference. That desire may be pragmatically useful for purposes of *negative* identification, but it does not provide much help for identifying actual organizations and relationships of human society that are diverse in character and purpose. Using the phrase "civil society," as Dionne and Barber do to refer to a "third sector" whose function is to mediate "between our specific individuality as economic producers and consumers and our abstract collectivity as members of a sovereign people," is both misleading and ultimately dehumanizing. Human identity is not adequately captured by the idea of a consuming/producing individual who only "abstractly" belongs to a sovereign collectivity and is thus "mediated" to that abstraction by a "third sector." No. Human beings have their identity as the image of God, created with an amazing range of responsibilities that can be realized only over many generations in the course of the historical differentiation and integration of all those capabilities and responsibilities in service to God. Healthy societies and a healthy globe, in other words, can be realized only by way of the proper differentiation, integration, and fulfillment of a diverse range of institutions and relationships, which require room—a common public space—in which justice is done to all. The just treatment of all, and the maintenance of the public square for all, are the responsibilities of public-legal governance.

What we need, then, is a normative framework for understanding and developing:

1. the proper historical differentiation and integration of human responsibilities in God's creation;
2. the proper exercise of the particular and necessary responsibility to govern an open, densely occupied, and highly interactive public square;

3. human identity as the image of God, resisting both the reduction of persons to their role as consumers, producers, and citizens, and the reduction of nongovernmental and non-economic organizations to a mere "mediating" function; and

4. the proper interlinking of all institutions and relationships in a just society.

Diverse Contexts

In her well-known book *Rights Talk*,[4] Harvard law professor Mary Ann Glendon argues that our American focus on the rights of individuals as the highest principle of law and politics makes it difficult, if not impossible, to obtain an adequate recognition and protection of "civil society." "Our legal and political vocabularies," she writes, "deal handily with rights-bearing individuals, market actors, and the state, but they do not afford us a ready way of bringing into focus smaller groups and systems where the values and practices that sustain our republic are shaped, practiced, transformed, and transmitted from one generation to the next" (120). What Glendon means by smaller groups and systems is "families, neighborhoods, workplace associations, and religious and other communities of obligation" (120). Other American theorists and social commentators have referred to these kinds of institutions and relationships as "mediating structures,"[5] "the social sector,"[6] the "third sector,"[7] "seedbeds of virtue,"[8] "a buffer,"[9] and simply "civil society."[10]

In European discourse, especially after the liberation of Eastern Europe from Soviet communist control, the phrase "civil society" has more often been used to refer to a narrower range of organizations and institutions—the ones that give people an organized public voice and identity over against totalitarian governments. The Catholic Church and Solidarity in Poland, for example, along with underground newspapers, civic organizations, and intellectual networks in Hungary, Czechoslovakia, and Russia, served as the seedbeds of revolution. Beyond Europe and America, both the public and the private meanings of "civil society" have been featured in discussions of Third World development.

A report from the International Jacques Maritain Institute in Rome, titled "Globalisation: A Challenge for Peace, Solidarity or Exclusion?"[11] highlights the "democratic deficit" inherent in the current process of globalization. The report calls for a new international social contract in which "the world is seen as a global civil society" (56). Fundamental to this reform, the report argues, are nongovernment organizations (NGOs) "which are not subject to political or economic interests and, more generally . . . are the bringers of human, religious, ethical and cultural values. . . . These are the institutions that normally help people to become aware of themselves, of their own values and their own most profound needs" (56). At a global level, the report goes on to say, "the organisations of civil society must be recognised and not authorised by governments." Furthermore, those organizations "must not stop at simply reporting wrongs and advocating solutions but must become true monitors of the activities of transnational companies and the international institutions" (58–59).

To conceive of civil society in these diverse ways poses difficulties, as we noted at the outset. In the view of some, the associations of "civil society" exist primarily to mediate between individuals and governments, or between individuals and the market. For others, their primary function is to serve as "seedbeds of virtue" or as seedbeds of citizenship. Still others emphasize the moral haven provided by these more intimate human communities in the context of an impersonal, perhaps even "un-virtuous" world of politics and market competition. Yet, if all of these meanings can be lodged in "civil society," is there no significance at all to the differences between a family and a political party, a church and a human rights watchdog organization, a service organization that feeds the hungry and a neighborhood?

Robert Putnam's widely broadcast argument in *Bowling Alone: The Collapse and Revival of American Community*[12] appears, at first glance, to address this question. There is an important difference, says Putnam, between two types of social capital. One is "bonding" (exclusive) and the other is "bridging" (inclusive) (22). Apart from the development of social capital, he says, political society will become ever more divided and people will retreat from tolerance and civic engagement. Americans now watch too much television instead of talking with their neighbors over the fence; they bowl alone instead of in leagues. Putnam's chief argument, however, is not that Americans should intensify the development of smaller, more intimate, nongovernmental "bonding" relationships for their own sake. Instead, he wants Americans to build "bridging" social capital, that is to increase their "connectedness" as citizens so that each person can feel included in the American community regardless of the private social and moral differences they may have. When, for example, Putnam calls for a new "great awakening," he is referring not to a spiritually deep evangelical revival, like those of America's past, but to a civic awakening that is "pluralistic" and "socially responsible." This means, among other things, that the goodness of any particular spiritual community should be judged by the extent to which it encourages its members to be "more tolerant of the faiths and practices of other Americans" (409).

Bonding in a family or religious community may, in fact, not even be good for the larger civic order, in Putnam's view, because that only "bolsters our narrower selves" (23). What America needs is more of the kind of bridging social capital that "can generate broader identities and reciprocity" (23). Bridging, as Putnam describes it, reflects and nurtures the highest value of liberal society, namely toleration, which amounts to each person respecting the other's autonomy in the broader society (350–363). Strong family and religious bonds may have a utilitarian value to the extent that they teach people to become tolerant of one another. However, if those institutions teach children to be intolerant of certain behaviors of other members of society, or train them, for example, to believe "narrowly" that the meaning of life is to be found in giving oneself wholeheartedly to Jesus Christ, then they may prove to be counterproductive to the building up of the bridging type of social capital that Putnam believes is so essential for our modern society (362–363). Putnam admits that much evidence points to the mutually reinforcing character of bonding and bridging social capital: "those who reach out to friends and family are often the most active in community outreach as well" (362). But this is not always the case. "Some kinds of bonding social capital may discourage the formation of bridging social capital and vice versa. That's what happened in the case of busing" (362).[13]

From the standpoint of the normative framework we are seeking, Putnam's argument reduces bonding social capital to a means—a means to the end of bridging social capital, which is the role he praises for "civil society." However, if American society is in danger of disintegrating under the impact of individualism and self-seeking, then to encourage individuals to be more publicly tolerant of other self-seeking individuals does not look like much of an answer to the problem. A political order that exists primarily to promote the social norm of individual autonomy and the market norm of consumer satisfaction may be able to maintain itself for a while as long as everyone can rely on healthy bonding social capital built up in the past. But how does bridging social capital help to restore the bonding relationships on which it depends?[14]

Some NGOs do indeed appear primarily to serve a bridging, or connecting, or mediating purpose, organizing individuals for civic or public-influence purposes. No doubt certain of these NGOs need to be strengthened in the United States and around the world today. However, the family and the church appear to have an original, internal, exclusive identity and purpose that is not reducible to a mediational or bridging purpose. Moreover, from a Christian vantage point these institutions are essential to the healthy identity of human beings and are not simply a means to other ends. Putnam has not given us much help to specify the identity of "civil society" or to explain how the diverse institutions and relationships of society ought to hold together.

More Than Means-to-End

If, instead of emphasizing the negative reference and the means-to-end role of "civil society," we were to consider each so-called social-sector institution and relationship in its own right, what would we look for and what would we find?

The wide variety of social bonds displays quite different types in terms of their commitments, obligations, sizes, purposes, and degrees of intensity, cooperation, and endurance. If there is any common denominator among them, it would appear to be simply that all are human and social. Yet that denominator does not distinguish them from political and economic institutions. Businesses and political communities are also human even if the obligations that obtain in those spheres are different in kind from the obligations that hold for families, friendships, and churches. It seems quite illegitimate, then, to describe NGOs in particular (as the report from the Jacques Maritain Institute does) as "bringers" of human, ethical, and cultural values, implying that political and economic institutions do not also do the same. At this point, therefore, we need to step back to ask why the "civil-society" question has been posed the way it has in the West and whether an appeal to the virtues of "civil society" is adequate, for example, to help guide social, economic, and political development in less-developed countries (LDCs).

Consider first the argument of Amartya Sen in *Development as Freedom*.[15] Sen contends that the direction of the West's "development" should itself be questioned. We should not simply assume that the West has arrived and has provided for all people of all time the normative meaning of social, economic, and political development. Among other things, Sen rejects the idea that some activities or institutions serve simply and chiefly as the means to the higher end of economic or political development. Instead, he contends that development ought to be conceived as the expansion of human freedom or "agency" and not primarily as a means of bringing remedial help to "patients." This leads to his argument in favor of developing human *capabilities*—the "substantive freedom" that makes it possible for people to "lead the lives they have reason to value and to enhance the real choices they have" (293). This is different from developing human *capital*, understood primarily as "augmenting production possibilities" (293). The goal of development is freedom, as Sen sees it, and not simply obtaining more goods and services.

While economic prosperity helps people to have wider options and to lead more fulfilling lives, so do more education, better health care, finer medical attention, and other factors that causally influence the effective freedoms that people actually enjoy. These "social developments" must directly count as "developmental," since they help us to lead longer, freer and more fruitful lives, in addition to the role they have in promoting productivity or economic growth or individual incomes (295).

From Sen's point of view we might say that pursuing economic and democratic development in LDCs so that individuals can have a higher level of income and enjoy the protection of individual rights is insufficient as a development goal. The pursuit of those ends at all cost may actually lead to the degrading of human life and community in other respects. Strengthening families, schools, voluntary associations, medical care, and civic action should be seen as ends in themselves because they expand and express human capabilities. If this is true, however, it takes us back to the original question about what constitutes "civil society" and whether that phrase even identifies a meaningful aggregate. It also heightens the importance of our concern with human identity. Sen is clearly trying to find a way to overcome an economic reductionist view of human beings that treats them as little more than producers and consumers. But who are human beings and what should their development aim for?

Return with me for a moment to the United States. Organizational development guru Peter Drucker discovered the importance of what he calls the "social sector" in the process of evaluating the development of western organizational management and economic change.[16] "Before the First World War," says Drucker, "farmers composed the largest single group in every country" (54). Today, "*productive* farmers make up less than half of the total farm population" and "no more than two percent of the work force" in the West" (54). The second-largest group in western populations around 1900 were live-in servants. Today there are scarcely any live-in domestic servants in the developed countries. The transformation that has taken place is, of course, the fruit of the Industrial Revolution. Yet that revolution was brief. "No class in history has ever risen faster than the blue-collar worker. And no class in history has ever fallen faster" (56). In the first decade of the twenty-first century, says Drucker, industrial workers in countries with well-developed free-market societies will shrink to constitute only an eighth of the work force. Today a new "knowledge society" is emerging along with an expanding service economy. Add to this the increasing mobility of people everywhere and one can easily understand why there are fewer and fewer of the older human relationships that were constituted by local community, extended family, and neighborhood. In other words, the institutions of an older society in the West are disappearing.

Who then attends to, or will attend to, the needs once met by local communities, families, and neighborhoods, Drucker asks. Everyone is now part of a larger organization, whether in their work or their private lives. Moreover, women are working, so the older, voluntary, and often informal human services rendered mostly by women who were not employed in the market economy have almost disappeared. Two answers to this question about community well-being and the service of people's needs were proposed in the twentieth century, says Drucker. The first answer was government: through the welfare state, government would meet the needs once met by local communities or "civil society." Although Drucker does not say so, this was also the answer assumed to be correct for LDCs by many western foreign-aid plans in the 1960s and 1970s.

The second answer, according to Drucker, was that the workplace community or corporate organization would meet the human needs once supplied by earlier forms of more personal community. For a time, this was also assumed by the West to be the answer to the question about Third World development: large-scale economic development would supply jobs and countless human benefits would trickle down to all.

However, both answers proved to be wrong or at least insufficient, Drucker concludes. "The right answer to the question Who takes care of the social needs and challenges of the knowledge society? is neither the government nor the employing organization. The answer is a separate and new *social sector*" (75). In the United States this third, nonprofit sector is composed mostly of religious organizations, but not churches. These organizations aim to change human beings, to create health and well-being. They also "serve a second and equally important purpose. They create citizenship" (76).

Whether or not Drucker is right about the identity and role of the "social sector" in the West, and particularly whether such a sector is *new*, one can see how he came to discover it. Drucker takes a fairly utilitarian approach to development, and the social sector is the source of certain important human services (for "patients," Sen would say). The "new" social sector has emerged, in Drucker's view, as a *means* to an old end, namely, to meet needs left unmet or left behind by ongoing technological, economic, and political developments, which are the chief motors of social change and ought not to be stopped. Yet here we need to turn Sen's argument around in order to question Drucker: is it not the case that economic, political, and social-sector organizations *all* meet human needs—the need for jobs, the need to develop one's talents, the need for police protection, transportation, and intellectual development? We may question whether the direction of western development has been healthy and whether economic growth should be expected to

take the lead, but surely the economic and political sectors as well as the social sector are arenas of interdependent human development.

Keeping in mind the contrasting arguments of Sen and Drucker, let's now
draw in Jean Bethke Elshtain to the discussion. Her assessment of the family
in relation to modern political development in the West is crucial at this
juncture. Democracy, Elshtain explains, arose out of opposition to kings and
chiefs and other traditional, unchosen, patriarchal authorities.[17] Ideals of
equality and hopes of self-government gradually took hold. But what also
took hold was a questioning of any and all traditional bonds—those bonds of
social life not contracted or freely chosen by individuals. That is the history
of modern, secularizing liberalism. Yet how do individuals achieve sufficient
maturity to become rational and self-governing, Elshtain asks. They do so
only by growing up in families from helpless infancy. And the family is one
of the most traditional and undemocratic institutions of society. That is why,
from Plato onward, those with ideas about radically redesigning society and
government have had to fight the family. This presents a problem, however,
for those who most want to build a society composed of autonomous individuals. If children do not experience strong, loving, parental authority in
families, they will not become independent adults. "Families are not democratic polities," says Elshtain, yet any "further erosion of that ethical life em-
bodied in the family bodes ill for democracy" (56). The crisis produced by
western individualism, she writes, is that the very foundation for the development of mature persons is being undermined in the quest for greater freedom and independence of those individuals. "Located inside a wider ethos
that no longer affords clear-cut moral and social support for familial relations
and responsibilities, young people, unsurprisingly, choose in growing numbers to postpone or evade these responsibilities" (57). Like Michael Sandel,
who criticizes the faulty liberal ideal of the "unencumbered self,"[18] and like
Glendon, who tracks the same history of liberalism to the apparent triumph
of individualist "rights talk," Elshtain rejects as illusory the ideal that democracy and free markets can survive without undemocratic institutions
such as the family.

Does this mean that Elshtain is simply nostalgic for an earlier period in
history, prior to the Industrial Revolution, when most people lived in small
towns and on family farms? No, to the contrary, she supports the ongoing
development and differentiation of society and of human responsibilities.
The family should not be absolutized any more than the democratic polity
should be absolutized. In actually nurturing children to adulthood, Elshtain
explains, families teach "that no authority on this earth is omnipotent, un-
changing, and absolute."[19] A proper democratic attitude toward society "in-

volves a rejection of any ideal of political and familial life that absorbs all social relations under a single authority principle" (56). Nothing should be absolutized and nothing made to serve only as a means to other ends, Elshtain implies.

To those who criticize her for being nostalgic for an earlier time, Elshtain responds by challenging the "triumphant progressivism" of her critics.[20] Triumphant progressives are those who refuse "to come to grips with the fact that federal-government-centered solutions don't solve all problems or even, more disturbingly, that not all of our problems are fixable. . . . [M]any of our troubles are troubles that will plague any mass postindustrial democracy. Civil society isn't so much about problem solving as about citizen and neighbor creating."[21] "Civil society," says Elshtain, "reminds us that this is a world of ties that bind. You cannot have all the good things of democratic life and culture without accountability and duty."[22] Without families, schools, churches, unions, and all the rest, including state and local governments, "there is no democratic culture and, indeed, nothing for the federal government to either correct or curb or serve."[23]

From Elshtain's point of view we can draw the conclusion that the historical differentiation and development of diverse social, economic, and political institutions is essential for the full realization of human life. At the same time, exclusive bonds cannot be replaced by "bridging" connections among free citizens. Strong, undemocratic families are essential to an open society. All of this has important implications for development strategies in more traditional societies that may still be dominated by family and clan ties. In those countries where exclusive family and clan bonds are still the strongest, governments often cannot or will not rule in the public interest in a disinterested fashion. They do not encourage the differentiation of independent social institutions and voluntary organizations. Instead, many such governments are authoritarian autocrats who rule in their own interest and in the interest of those closely related to them. The political order has not become sufficiently differentiated from the rest of society and strong enough to fulfill a responsibility of upholding equal justice for all. It does not function to "correct or curb or serve" all citizens in the full diversity of their social and economic life.

Alan Whaites makes the same point, that the celebration of the decline of the state in parts of Africa, for example, has been a mistake.[24] The government of a weak state that is unable to keep competing groups apart and dedicated to a larger common good creates a highly dangerous situation because "civil society" groups in many Third World countries are based on "primordial identity." Proliferation of conflict throughout the 1990s, says

Whaites, fed on these identities that became the focus for entirely selfish group competition (143). Of course, to make a critical judgment like this implies not only a normative standard for government; it also implies a normative rationale for the ongoing differentiation of societies so that a greater diversity of human capabilities can be realized. Family or clan independence must not be the highest development goal of human society.

What is gradually emerging from our conversation with these diverse commentators is an initial outline of a normative framework for evaluating healthy human development. People the world over need to achieve sustainable balance among multiple, differentiating responsibilities, some of which can be fulfilled only through independent institutions and organizations, each of which needs to be developed in accord with its distinctive purpose. In other words, to affirm healthy societal differentiation is to reject the idealization of older, less-differentiated social, political, and economic communities. In order for ongoing historical development to occur, it is essential that impartial, public-legal authorities (governments) emerge to govern political communities in which independent, nongovernment institutions and organizations are recognized and protected.

To argue in this way obviously entails making normative judgments about what constitutes a just political community, a sound economy, and a healthy society. Societal differentiation, in other words, does not by itself guarantee the normative development of each differentiated institution. The more kinds of responsibility people have, the more ways they can do what is wrong as well as what is right. One of the aims of the normative framework we are seeking, therefore, is to avoid or to overcome the absolutization of the family, the state, the market, and the individual in order to promote societal differentiation and integration in a well-balanced and just fashion. If a healthy society needs both undemocratic families and a democratic government, both disciplined schools and profit-making enterprises, both strongly encumbered selves and free-choice consumers, then how do we derive the norms for all of these different relationships and institutions? If each institution has its own character and none should be all-embracing or omnicompetent, then what ought to be the right balance and relation among them? How ought they to be both differentiated in their own right and integrated together in harmonious societies and a just global order? Underlying all of these questions, certainly, is the question about the meaning and purpose of human life in its entirety. These are the big questions—the questions of greatest importance—not only for development in the South but also for development and reform in the North.

Seeking Biblical Wisdom for Human Development

It should be evident by this point that the questions we are asking and the criticisms we are leveling arise from a Christian point of view. But let's take the initial exploration further and ask more pointedly what is entailed in a Christian view of human development. Biblically speaking, the meaning and value of family life, of the education of children and adults, of the service of neighbors in need, of the work of medical and other professions, and of organizational efforts to promote justice in society—the meaning and value of these is *not*, first of all, that they are means to the end of economic growth or democratic government. The pressure to orient all of life toward the economic and political maximization of human freedom, for example, distorts the real meaning of human life in *all* spheres, including the economic and the political. Economic growth for the sake of more consumption, and politics reduced to rights talk also represent distorted forms of economic and political life. So the aim of social recovery and healthy development, from a Christian-democratic point of view, must not be simply to strengthen so-called seedbeds of virtue and watchdogs of government so that the market and democracy can survive. Instead, the aim must be the reformation of all of life through orientation of every sphere to its true purpose.

If the full meaning of human life cannot be properly realized apart from service to neighbors, apart from the development of musical talent, teamwork in scientific laboratories, apart from the worship of God, and apart from the deep intimacy of human friendships, marriages, and multigenerational family life, then all of the activities and organizations that are necessary to realize these ends must be seen as meaningful in their own right. This is what development should mean in any country or culture in the world.

Economic development and democracy should therefore be viewed in this larger context of human meaning. A society in which an open market allows for more human entrepreneurship and creative activity is a society in which more human talents can be developed and interrelated. A society in which the political authorities are held accountable by citizens to protect their rights to speak, to worship, and to pursue many different human activities, is a society in which a greater number of dimensions of human life can develop simultaneously. In this sense, democratic politics and open markets both *aid* and *express* human development. Consequently, commerce, industry, politics, and government are themselves meaningful, God-given dimensions of human-life-in-community and not merely the means to other ends or the evils to be curbed by "civil society." Those with gifts in the art of sales, industrial organizing, advertising, political organizing, conflict resolution, and public administration are called to develop important human talents and fulfill valuable human aspirations in those avenues of service. The chief question behind all human development, therefore, is this: what is the purpose of human life and how should the different dimensions of human experience be developed simultaneously and interdependently in order for humans adequately to realize their identity as the image of God?

Amartya Sen speaks of human beings as needing not simply more "utilities" or "primary goods," but as needing more "substantive freedoms"—"capabilities . . . to choose a life one has reason to value" (74). There is a diversity of human "functionings" that needs to be kept in view with regard to substantive freedom, he argues. Consequently, a "person's 'capability' refers to the alternative combinations of functionings that are feasible for her to achieve. Capability is thus a kind of freedom: the substantive freedom to achieve alternative functioning combinations (or, less formally put, the freedom to achieve various lifestyles)" (75). Now, Sen has hit on something important here. Nevertheless, he has done so in an inadequate way. While trying to be empirical in one respect, his attempt to generalize with value-neutral terms leads to an abstraction from the real *valuational* struggle in which humans are always engaged. The fact is that some people want to pursue wealth above all else while others choose a lifestyle of poverty. Some discover musical talent within themselves and others do not. Some decide to balance many "functionings" of work, family life, voluntary service, hobbies, and recreation while others give themselves to only one cause. Some value community most highly; some seek to live with few if any obligations to others. Why are humans like this? How should we judge what is good and bad about any of these lifestyles? How do people with different talents benefit one another? Sen's abstractions of "capabilities" and "functionings" do not adequately address these questions and do not help to illuminate standards by which to judge normative and anti-normative functionings.

The concern about moral standards and not just about freedom and functionings is one of Gertrude Himmelfarb's chief concerns with respect to the loose use of the term "civil society." What is required today, she argues, "is not only a restoration of civil society but the far more difficult task of reformation—moral reformation. Even to articulate the problem is difficult, because the language of morality has become suspect. One of the reasons the idea of civil society is so attractive is that it is couched in the language of sociology."[25] From a Christian-democratic point of view, then, what are the foundations for a moral viewpoint, for the language of moral judgments about normative and anti-normative development patterns?

It is possible, I believe, to keep meat on the bones abstracted by sociological and economic analyses and to speak about human obligations quite concretely if we speak in terms of "talents," "callings," and "responsibilities" rather than in terms of "functionings" and "capabilities." God has constituted human beings with many different talents and callings with which to respond to one another and to the One in whose image they have been created. All human responsibilities, ultimately, represent a response to God. The image of God—male and female, in their generations—is a complex creature *called* to fill the earth and to develop the whole creation in order to know and praise God and thereby to come to true self-knowledge as the image of God in community. The ability to make music, pursue agriculture, build bridges, fly to the moon, raise a child, write public laws, nurture love in an intimate friendship, invent millions of types of machines, and play in the backyard or on a stage—all of these and much, much more *reveal something about both God and the image of God*. To develop any of these human talents or interests properly is to pursue a calling from God. And the pursuit of such callings both depends on and requires service to, and cooperation with, fellow humans and other creatures. In fact, when properly analyzed, every talent and calling is to one degree or another a shared, communal activity exercised in response to normative standards that bind creatures to one another and to their Creator in a covenant relationship.

Talents and callings are not merely the functionings or capabilities of free individual selves, as if freedom has an original, creative meaning prior to, or apart from, those talents and responsibilities given by God. Neither "civil society" nor any other part of human life is merely a realm we create for ourselves. The variety of human callings are constitutive of the image of God who exists only in complete dependence on God. Altogether the diverse kinds of abilities and exercises of human responsibility arise from a depth that is nothing less than the revelatory connection—the covenant communion—between God and the image of God. Humans have their identity as the image of God, and everything they are and do reveals something about that deepest source and meaning of life. Sen's phrase "substantive freedom" is thus an abstraction that allows for very limited normative content. The content that he gives it throughout his book comes from the fact that he is exploring dimensions of creaturely life on earth that must be accounted for in terms of an origin and a destiny that can only be grasped by humans in communion with God. And the modes of that communion in this age are not just prayer and worship, but include a full life of earthly stewardship, service, and development. Thus, *human development may be defined as the unfolding, diversifying, and complexifying exercise of all the responsibilities that belong to the generations of the image of God, and this occurs in a healthy fashion only when humans steward the earth creatively with all of their talents in obedience to and in fellowship with the One who has called them into service toward the destiny of face to face fellowship with God.*

From this point of view it becomes possible to see why economic development is itself an important and essential human calling, but one that, if absolutized or distorted, can cripple other aspects of human development as well as the very meaning of stewardly enterprise. From this point of view, one can see how crucial a just political system is if humans are to achieve the right public-legal integration of a differentiating society. A just political order must accomplish more than merely the protection of individual freedom and an open market. The public square is more than a market. Likewise, authoritarian governments, which serve the interests of one family or clan, of one interest or another, must also be judged inadequate and even dangerous for human well-being in differentiating societies. Governments that deny people the right to exercise God-given responsibilities to educate their children, to worship as their conscience leads them, or to organize freely, are governments that inhibit genuine human development.

If either government or the market in a given society, or at the global level, suppresses human responsibility in other spheres of life, one can understand why the hope has arisen in some circles that "civil society" might be able to save the world. For it is certainly true that if the richness of human creativity and responsibility is nurtured among people in a healthy, balanced way, there will, over time, be positive economic and political consequences. Nevertheless, these positive consequences do not follow naturally or inevitably. Economic and political responsibilities must themselves be exercised in normative ways to help realize properly balanced patterns of development.[26]

Conclusion

Although the implications of the foregoing discussion are vast in number, the confines of this chapter will allow for only a brief outline of a few of them.

1. The historical emergence of impartial or disinterested governments, called to govern political communities with "justice for all," is a development that must go hand in hand with the differentiation of other institutions and associations, including some form of economic marketplace. "Civil society" cannot save a people from oppressive, unjust governments, but neither can such governments be changed without

the emergence of a sense of civic purpose and the ability of citizens to mobilize in order to reform or replace oppressive governments. For the latter to occur, people need to become literate, publicly engaged, and willing to act in the public interest, and this is where many "civil-society" institutions and organizations of a mediating type come in. Opening free markets and opening a society to foreign investment will not inevitably lead to just governments and a flourishing "civil society" that includes a free press, independent political parties, and so forth. As with all historical development, however, well-balanced societal differentiation and integration never occur without the opening of markets for free exchange. So the question will always be one of how to bring balanced social, economic, and political development where it does not exist. In that sense, the aim to encourage the development of a variety of "civil-society" institutions in poor countries, which currently may be overcontrolled by arbitrary, authoritarian governments and/or by domestic or international economic forces, should be pursued with utmost diligence. Political and economic changes in themselves are not sufficient, nor will the reform of those public institutions be possible without the multidimensional social development of the people. Michael Walzer makes this point well when he says,

> The network of associations incorporates, but it cannot dispense with, the agencies of state power; neither can socialist cooperation or capitalist competition dispense with the state. . . . Citizenship is one of the many roles that members [of society] play, but the state itself is unlike all the other associations. It both frames civil society and occupies space within it. It fixes the boundary conditions and the basic rules of all associational activity.
>
> Only a democratic state can create a democratic civil society; only a democratic society can sustain a democratic state. The civility that makes democratic politics possible can only be learned in the associational networks; the roughly equal and widely dispersed capabilities that sustain the networks have to be fostered by the democratic state.[27]

2. The work of NGOs should not be thought of as necessarily in conflict or in tension with economic organizations and a free market, such that NGOs have to save people from markets and corporations. A mistaken absolutization of capitalism or of the goal of economic growth will certainly distort human communities and associations that are not economically or politically qualified. But those distortions are a sign of a faulty, anti-normative development of the economy and of the laws

that govern business and the economy. The fact is that an open society with an open market is one of the important constituents of human flourishing. Without such freedom of exchange, many of the talents and callings that belong to people will not be able to be developed and interwoven with one another. The moral import here is that the *simultaneous* development of healthy, limited markets *and* of healthy families, schools, voluntary associations, and social-action organizations is necessary, with each being developed in accord with its own normative purpose.[28]

3. With respect to both a healthy political community and a healthy market we might use the analogy of a choir or orchestra, as long as we don't stretch the analogy too far. It takes many different voices, many different kinds of instruments, to make certain kinds of music. Each voice or instrument needs to be developed in accord with its own character and purpose. Not everyone can aspire to be the soloist or the conductor. This is not to suggest that a government, stock market, or central bank is the conductor of a single social purpose (a single piece of music), because the public-legal interweaving of society or the simultaneous movement of many market exchanges is more complicated and diversified than a musical concert. The point of the analogy, however, is to say that a government which suppresses families, the media, and/or political advocacy will distort human life for everyone, much like a conductor would destroy a symphony if he or she refused to allow the violins to come on stage and made the horns play the parts of the woodwinds. A market that allowed only multinational corporations to participate and denied a place to nonprofit organizations would be like a choir with a very limited repertoire that kept many potential vocalists and instrumentalists from ever being able to develop their talents.

4. An important note about "self-interest" and "selfishness" must also be entered here. Sometimes the market and economic enterprising as well as interest-group politics, and even government itself, are viewed as selfish and self-serving, while "civil-society" efforts are valued as constructive because they are oriented toward the good of others and not self-serving. A corporation's aim to make a profit is seen as self-serving, while the aim of a nonprofit job-training program is seen as other-serving. "Civil society" is the "good guy" who will, in this context, save the world from the clutches of the "bad guy"—the evil corporations and governments of this world. These distinctions harbor both truths and falsehoods, but they do not help clarify the norms that hold for different institutions and relationships. Consider the following examples.

a. Parents in a family legitimately bear responsibility for their children. It is not selfish, then, for them to look after the interests of their children and of their family. When questions of public policy arise that touch on the family, nothing could be more legitimate than for parents to want those public policies to be good for *their* children. Love of one's own children, like proper self-love, is not illegitimate. It is one of the bases for learning how to love others as ourselves. Where selfishness supplants proper self-love and love of one's own, however, is when parents seek *only* the benefit of their children and do not rise beyond that motivation to see that they and their children are also neighbors, citizens, and friends of others, including other children. Public policies or neighborhood watch groups must serve all families and all children, and there is always a point at which true parental love must show itself by the way parents teach their children to love others, sometimes sacrificially and regardless of themselves.

b. For a business to try to increase its sales or to seek adequate legal protection and the best tax policies for its own benefit is not selfish or greedy. Only by producing and selling its product in an encouraging environment can it employ people, serve customers, and do all kinds of other good things. That is what a business does to fulfill its own purpose and to be of service to others. Yet if the only thing business people do is to seek the interest of their own businesses and lobby for benefits to help their businesses regardless of all else, then they turn proper self-care into unjust and unstewardly selfishness. They fail to see that in their civic capacity, for example, they should be seeking justice for all businesses, all laborers, all citizens, all nonprofit organizations, and the environment. Even within their businesses there is more to success than self-service. As Sen comments, it is incorrect "to conclude that the success of capitalism as an economic system depends only on self-interested behavior, rather than on a complex and sophisticated value system that has many other ingredients, including reliability, trust, and business honesty (in the face of contrary temptations)."[29]

The myth of the "invisible hand" has become, for many people, a political philosophy that confuses the legitimacy of businesses pursuing their own ends with the idea that the public good is best achieved only as an indirect outcome of everyone seeking their own interests. The element of truth in this "myth" is that if every family nurtures love within itself, if every school succeeds at its teaching, if every business is stewardly and productive in its own quest for success in a free market, and if every voluntary association tends to its own purpose diligently, then all of this will add up to something good for everyone. But the element of error in the myth is the assumption that the common good of the entire public order can be achieved indirectly without anyone paying attention to it or nurturing it directly for its own sake. This is mistaken. A political community has its own calling, its own offices, its own purposes, its own normative standards of justice for the public square. The health of the political order is not guaranteed as an indirect consequence of the action of other organizations and institutions even when the others behave normatively in their own spheres. There is more to the common good than an accumulation of multiple private goods. And, in fact, no differentiated private good can be achieved outside the context of a public-legal governance structure that upholds and protects it.

c. Internationally, there is nothing wrong with states seeking to protect their own national interests. After all, governments have primary responsibility for their own citizens; they do not govern the citizens of other countries. But here again, if everything a government does is oriented only toward its own interests, narrowly conceived, regardless of what is good for other states or the international order, it will fail to take seriously the responsibility it bears—*together with other states*—to do justice internationally and transnationally. Governments, in other words, are no more free, in God's creation, to be entirely self-occupied within their own borders than are people within their own homes or businesses. God's purposes for human beings and the responsibilities they have do not allow for the absolutization of state sovereignty. Proper self-regard and self-care of states amounts to something different than nationalistic self-preoccupation and self-centeredness. And in a shrinking globe it becomes more and more apparent with each passing day that the national interests of any state depend very much on a healthy and just world order.

d. While it is true that the institutions and organizations of "civil society" tend to be viewed as worthy *empowerment* vehicles, they themselves can act in selfish, unjust ways that are bad both for people and for the larger society. A desire to protect the environment, for example, does not guarantee the wisdom and justice of every lobby effort by environmentalists, particularly if they do not recognize that governments must deal with more than environmental protection. Families that fail at being families do not thereby serve as seedbeds of virtue. "The family, the most basic and intimate unit of civil society," says Himmelfarb, "is hardly a paragon of virtue."[30] Those who serve the poor with job training or financial support can do so in misguided ways that instill in recipients a sense of victimhood or of class hatred. Whaites makes the point that NGOs in the Third World tend to see the world made better "by 'scaling up' their own areas of expertise, usually leading to a lack of appreciation of the macro-environment by which their own and everybody else's issues are shaped."[31] The diversity and lack of accountability of some NGOs, when coupled with weak political institutions, can create obstacles to the constructive work of NGOs. Just as political and economic institutions need to develop in accord with normative standards, so also must all other organizations.

The aim of social analysis and responsible action, therefore, must be to clarify and heed the norms or standards that should guide those who bear responsibility in families, schools, businesses, nonprofit organizations, and governments. Only by means of the normative development of each such institution and organization *simultaneously* and *together* can a healthy and just society be sustained and further developed. "Civil society" cannot save the world, but people who respond to God obediently to build just states, to nurture loving families, to perfect good schools, to meet the real needs of the poor and handicapped, and to build sound, stewardly businesses can, together, by God's grace, give evidence of the whole creation being renewed.

5. Finally, the differentiation of society, which includes the development of countless talents and callings in thousands of fields of music, art, industry, commerce, science, technology, education, leisure, government and politics, means increasing opportunities for every person to use his or her gifts. And this should be as true for women as it is for men. One of the important fruits of social differentiation and public-legal integration is that people can exercise many different responsibilities all at the same time. Less differentiated societies often have fixed and relatively few roles for individuals. It has been possible in different societies at different points in history to think in terms of permanent classes and gender roles. Yet even with a high view of marriage as a life-long, intimate bond and of family as the most fundamental of social relationships, one can see that the marital and family

roles do not exhaustively define women any more than they exhaustively define men. With changes in employment patterns, social attitudes, and public laws, it becomes possible within relatively well-balanced, differentiated societies for women as well as men to enter into marriage and build strong families while also developing a diverse range of talents and fulfilling diverse responsibilities outside the home. Insofar as we see men and women together as the image of God, called to serve God with all that they are and have, we must seek diligently to make it possible for every person, in community, to develop and bring to light their gifts and abilities.

CHAPTER THREE

The Question of Being Human

Progress or Regress?

Do we know more or less today about what it means to be human? On the face of it this question sounds foolish. Who can doubt that we know much more today about human experience than people knew fifty or one hundred or five hundred years ago? The sciences are still developing, and they provide us with new data every year; people continue to explore everything in the cosmos, including themselves, and they learn new things every day; human inventiveness and creativity show no sign of letting up. Speaking both quantitatively and qualitatively, it appears that humans know more today than ever before in history about what it means to be human.

Despite all the gains in knowledge and experience, however, much evidence suggests that regress has also occurred over the centuries in at least some dimensions of human experience and self-understanding. Abuse, torture, and slaughter of fellow humans, new diseases and causes of death, political injustice, individual hopelessness and suicide—all of these were more abundant in the twentieth century than in any earlier century. It seems clear, therefore, that to assess the evidence of progress and regress we will have to choose carefully the point of view from which to make such judgments.

If, for instance, we assume that human identity and behavior patterns can eventually be explained exhaustively by means of the natural sciences, and if we also assume that whatever cannot be known scientifically is not so important, then we might read a great deal into the "progress" of science during the past two hundred years. Scientists do know more today than they did fifty years ago about stimulus-response patterns, psycho-physical disorders, mass psychology, group dynamics, and countless other aspects of human behavior.

If, by contrast, we assume that human beings are more than psycho-biological animals and that the quality of human life and self-understanding must be measured, at least in part, by the depth of practical human wisdom and the depth and breadth of moral, political, legal, and aesthetic experience humans enjoy, then a great deal of ambiguity comes into view. We must then take careful notice of the signs of increasing degradation of human life—suicide and murder rates, levels of child abuse, malnutrition, and starvation, rates of divorce and joblessness, the destructiveness of wars and other episodes of organized brutality. Some critics judge that a great deal of art and music, literature and journalism, legal thinking and ecclesiastical life are of a lower quality today than they were two or three centuries ago. Many wonder whether human beings as religious, moral, and political creatures have made any progress at all.

The late Eric Voegelin, to take just one example, develops his political philosophy around the argument that the differentiation and expansion of human experience from the ancient Hebrews and Greeks through the European Middle Ages displayed a certain kind of expansion of human self-understanding and wisdom, a progress in the experience of what it means to be human in relation to God and fellow human beings.[1] With the growing impact of modern scientism, and the application of natural scientific methods to human studies, however, Voegelin argues that human society has been experiencing a regression in self-understanding because the reductionistic mind-set leads to a forgetfulness or loss of consciousness about the profound meaning of life. We may know more today than our ancestors knew about certain bodily and psycho-social functions, Voegelin would say, but we have a shallower and more derailed knowledge of ourselves as moral, intellectual, aesthetic, and social creatures. We hold less of the truth and we hold it less firmly; the deeper meaning of life has become more opaque to us and marked increasingly by uncertainty and confusion. We are less richly human now than our ancestors were. Humans today have lost or forgotten a great deal of what our ancestors once knew and experienced.[2]

One need not adopt Voegelin's point of view to have some sense that all is not well in the arena of experiencing what it means to be human. The question of being human is not narrowly about how many discrete details we can learn about various human functions and activities. The broader, more basic question concerns human identity as a whole, from the inside, and at its foundations. This includes the personal, existential questions that each of us asks not as a scientific observer but as a living person: Who am I? What is the meaning of life? To what purposes should I give myself? How do I arrive at answers to questions like these? Depending on how one answers these questions, all the diverse functions and activities of human life will appear in different lights. Moreover, no one can wait until all the "facts" are in to decide how to live and what it means to be human. One must live today and tomorrow on the basis of assumptions and beliefs about what it means to be human. My presuppositions, whether correct or incorrect, will guide not only the way I seek to learn about human life but also the way I choose to live and make decisions.

If one lives and interprets life's meaning based on the belief that human beings have been created in the image of God and that in all of their relationships and responsibilities they are marked to the core by their relation to God, then one's point of view will be radically different from the view that human meaning is confined within the course of natural, animal cycles without a transcendent origin, reference point, or meaning. These contrasting points of view, to name just two, can lead to significantly different judgments about what is good and bad in contemporary society and about the proper aim of public policies to affect what is good and bad.

Why, for example, do we, or should we, believe that something is wrong when people are locked into poverty, crime, ill health, and hopelessness? Why not assume that some people are simply fated for such lives? Nature is harsh at times. Evolutionary destiny requires the survival of the fittest. Some make it, some do not. Some rise to the top and others sink to the bottom. That is a simple, natural fact for humans just as it is for other animals. Obviously, to judge that certain living conditions are good or bad, acceptable or unacceptable, is to take for granted certain *standards* or *principles* by which to judge the quality and meaning of human life. But where do such standards come from, and which suppositions about human identity point us to the correct standards or principles? The fact that human beings can discuss such matters and make judgments in the course of deliberative argument would seem to suggest that we ought to reflect critically on our presuppositions, especially at a time when people throughout this shrinking globe hold such different religious and ideological convictions about the causes of poverty and war, on the one hand, and about the way to peace and social order, on the other.

Anthropological Presuppositions of Public Policy

Public policies in the United States, as we have known them for roughly the last fifty to sixty years, have been created by governments to try to promote certain human goods such as education, health care, and social stability for the elderly, and to overcome or to alleviate circumstances judged to be unhealthy or morally unacceptable such as racial discrimination, poverty, drug abuse, and out-of-wedlock births to young teenagers.[3] In creating such policies, governments have presumed that the personal relationships, families, nongovernment institutions, economic enterprises, and corporations in which people participate are insufficient to meet these needs. Government must take action. Generally speaking, one of the key standards of judgment undergirding government policies since the 1960s has been that no citizen should have to live below the poverty line without receiving material assistance from the government. Yet the assistance that government has sought to provide is minimum assistance and is not intended to be the complete answer to the needs and problems it addresses. American welfare policies, for example, have never had as their aim to try to make the poorest citizens as rich as the richest citizens or even as comfortable as middle-class citizens. Public welfare policies, if we ignore all the rhetoric, represent an extension of "poor relief," the attempt to alleviate joblessness, insufficient income, and helplessness in order to lift those in need from unacceptable poverty to acceptable poverty, but not up to middle-class comfort. Government's direct responsibility goes only so far.

Poor relief or welfare assistance comes on top of other laws and programs designed to sustain or improve the general welfare of all citizens: tax-supported education, income tax deductions for dependents, unemployment compensation for those temporarily unemployed, and more. Furthermore, the well-being of most citizens is generally assumed to be the consequence not of particular government efforts but of the responsible actions of individuals and families going about their daily tasks of working, child rearing, and studying, supported by family members, friendships, neighborhoods, churches, and places of employment.

Notice the web of assumptions about human identity and meaning here. Adults are presumed to be responsible social creatures, but government's judgments about their well-being are largely judgments about their relative economic positions and relative independence as individuals. Governments should presumably step in to help those in need without asking too much about how their predicament has come to pass and why other institutions and relationships have not been able to help them. Consequently, citizens and governments can feel that they have fulfilled their public responsibility to the poor as long as they have offered a few public benefits to help them reach the potential for a lower-class level of economic existence. Beyond that, the public does not need to feel any greater obligation. Many questions about other qualities of human life in society and about justice, love, and responsibility before God are left entirely unaddressed.

One of the curious facts about prevailing assumptions undergirding modern social policies is that the aim to increase individual freedom is interpreted in quite different ways even by those who start from the same assumptions. Many, for example, who emphasize the principle of *equality* (or at least fairness) among free individuals typically consider the poorest Americans to be in need of goods, services, and money that will allow them to live more like people who are not so poor. It is the considerable distance between wealth and poverty that pains them. Unequal outcomes offend them. On the other hand, many who stress the standard of equal *freedom* among individuals urge that poor people should be treated in ways that will help them become more accountable for their own actions—just as everyone else is treated. In other words, the gap of inequality in our society between responsibility and irresponsibility is what offends those who want people to act independently rather than dependently. If the truth about human identity is that people ought to be free, then let each person accept the responsibilities of freedom and the consequences of their action.

In the United States, we call the first group liberal and the second group conservative, but both believe in the *freedom* and *equality* of individuals. The difference arises from the accent they place on one of the two words and from the way they see government supporting their accented understanding of freedom and equality. Those with an equality-oriented viewpoint more often stress the economic/social conditions of inequality that keep poor people from enjoying a better standard of living. Those with a freedom-oriented perspective more often emphasize the behavioral habits that free individuals ought to learn and exhibit. Both groups may favor special government action on behalf of needy citizens, but the first will be more sympathetic to longer-term, public financial support of the poor without judging too closely the decisions those individuals make, while the second will be more sympathetic to temporary policies that help get individuals working again and off the dole.[4]

In both cases, however, similar assumptions about human nature and society are at work. The aim is the familiar liberal aim: to make people more free and equal—more autonomous as individuals and more equal, materially, in comparison to fellow citizens. The taken-for-granted context is that

of individuals functioning in a larger public order—a context in which unencumbered individuals should, ideally, be free to act on their own initiative and in which governments should act minimally to adjust the social
and economic outcomes to keep the poorest and those most at risk from
losing out altogether. Humans, from this point of view, are economically
acquisitive animals, destined to desire maximum individual autonomy
while also bearing a public-moral sense that is activated when the poorest
people have to endure circumstances that the middle classes do not find acceptable. This is all part of a classical liberal perspective on society.

Is something missing here? How do these hypothetically free human beings achieve the capability of acting autonomously? Do they create themselves? What is the nature of human growth and development from birth to
adulthood? How does it happen? Who is responsible for it? Do individuals
alone exist, and do they act in response to their moral conscience only
through government? Where do families, schools, churches, business enterprises, and voluntary organizations fit into this picture? For example, can human life develop in a healthy fashion outside the circle of an enduring family? With respect to the most basic assumptions about human identity, what
is the nature and meaning of family life? Is there a sense in which human beings are fundamentally interdependent family creatures before they become
acquisitive individuals and civic egalitarians?

I ask these questions not to imply that there is a self-evident answer to
them. Rather, the purpose of the questions is to suggest the opposite: the answers will be quite different depending on what one assumes, at bottom, to
be the meaning of human life. Additional questions can easily be added to
the list. Is there anything besides economic advancement, individual freedom, and material equality that properly motivates individuals and satisfies
their sense of purpose and well-being? Should freedom be thought of primarily as maximum individual autonomy—the maximum freedom to change
commitments in minimum time, to consume an ever-widening array of goods
and services, and to remain unbound by enduring institutional obligations?
Or is there something else humans must do in order to achieve fulfillment?
And what should we make of the fact that humans quite often violate the
standards of behavior they profess to accept? Individuals do not always appear to act even in their own best interests.

If we turn our attention from the individual to the larger society, we must
ask additional questions: Is equality really the primary public standard that
should weigh on human conscience? Or are there other standards that suffer
diminution if equality is overemphasized or absolutized?[5] Furthermore, if
equality is so important, why should we accept welfare policies that do little

more than lift people from underclass status to lower-class status? Why should government not lift all people to a condition of genuine equality? Do welfare recipients actually experience a greater sense of equality as a consequence of benefiting from welfare programs, or is the sense of equality felt only by those who design and deliver the welfare support?

All of these questions lead in a definite direction—to the following question: should the debate over social policies today be redirected instead to a debate over the presuppositions that give rise to the policies? If the standard operating policies by which government deals with education, health care, families, civil rights, employment security, social security, and crime are insufficient to maintain equality among all citizens and to keep those most at risk from dangerous predicaments, and if we still have not overcome or fundamentally alleviated poverty in the United States, then is it perhaps time to give greater attention to the basic assumptions we hold about government's responsibility? Could it be that the liberal presuppositions about human nature—about individual autonomy and civic equality—are so flawed and inadequate that they require radical revision or supplementation before we can even begin to engage in disputes over the finer points of various social policies?

If the answers to these questions are affirmative, as I believe they are, then it is incumbent upon us to turn a critical eye toward our fundamental assumptions and presuppositions about human identity and meaning in this world.

The Complexity of Human Identity

Today in the United States we live in a differentiated society. We no longer live in tight clans or on feudal estates in which decisions about everything in life fell under the authority of a single head. We no longer live in a society in which church and state alone were able to make the rules for every other relationship and institution. We experience life in a manifold of relatively independent organizations, institutions, and relationships. Families, churches, businesses, scientific and artistic organizations, universities, newspapers, book publishers, and thousands of nonprofit voluntary associations all follow their own courses, acting not at all as branches of government.

Even though liberal ideology interprets all institutions and relationships as artificial, that is, as reducible to contracts among supposedly autonomous individuals, the fact remains that many of the strongest and oldest social entities exhibit lives of their own, structuring and defining the behavior of individuals rather than the other way around. A publishing firm is something quite different from a farm; a church is quite distinct from an art club; a family has a character markedly different from a business enterprise. Each of these, with its own history of development, is a rich composite of received tradition, creative innovation, response to transcendent principles, and a sense of shared obligation.

The differentiated character of our social experience demonstrates the inadequacy of a political philosophy that reduces every human problem to the relative economic condition and equality (or inequality) of supposedly autonomous individuals. Individuals do not actually manifest self-sufficient, self-defining capabilities. To the contrary, in almost every situation in life individuals bear responsibility with and for one another in homes, schools, churches, employment, politics, and so forth. This is one of the reasons why the so-called communitarians criticize "rights talk" that has become abstracted from the responsibilities and obligations of real people in real communities and institutions.[6] There are very few rights one may legitimately claim and exercise that do not go hand in hand with obligations in and through a variety of organized relationships.

Moreover, on the responsibility side of this equation, it is not only the state and its laws to which one is accountable. Parents and children in a home bear responsibility for one another; church members and leaders bear responsibility for each other; employers and employees, teachers and students, friends and neighbors—all bear distinct types of mutual responsibility defined by the distinctive character of those relationships and institutions. A concern for the freedom and relative economic standing of citizens can never adequately lead to justice for citizens if it fails to take into account the fact that citizens are always *more than* citizens. Meaningful citizenship in a differentiated society depends on the fact that human beings exercise a variety of other (and often prior) responsibilities. The hypothetically autonomous individual who is supposed to be free to enjoy certain rights does not exist solely in relation to the state but also in relation to family members, neighbors, employer or employees, and more. The question, then, is How should public law take into account the full reality of human experience? Or to ask it in a different way, how should government do justice to citizens (political creatures) who are always more than citizens and who are not, in fact, autonomous individuals but thoroughly interdependent social creatures?

One cannot address these inescapable questions without revealing one's basic religious/philosophical assumptions. One cannot deal with the issues at stake without making (or presuming) a case for what humans are and how they *ought* to live. It has become more and more clear over the last two decades that the dispute over social welfare, for example, is caused by deeper

the image of God points beyond itself to the One in whose image human beings have been created.

The very fact that human creatures have come to different conclusions about their own identity shows that they are responsible creatures called to reflect, to choose, to make judgments, to draw conclusions, and to act on their convictions personally and in relation with others. Even when, in disobedience against God, human beings seek ultimate fulfillment in one or another creaturely function or earthly relationship rather than in God, they exhibit capabilities and qualities that inhere only in the image of God, not in other earthly creatures. God has given human beings real responsibility to shape life in this world, even to the point of their own destruction if their deeds are evil and misguided. Human beings shape both themselves and history; they are not merely shaped by others or by historical or genetic forces. They are not locked into a repetitive cycle of animal instincts that change little, if at all, over the generations. Humans are indeed social, familial, political, aesthetic, scientific, playful creatures, but they have an underlying, integrating wholeness about them that cannot be reduced to any one of these institutions, abilities, or characteristics.

To confess that human beings have been created in the image of God means discovering that the center of gravity of human life cannot be found in any single human relationship, institution, or role, but only in God. We have been created ultimately for fellowship with God—for an eternal destiny—and as Augustine said, we will remain restless until we find our rest in God. If life reveals its true meaning in this light, then human responsibility entails working out the meaning and limited purpose of each relationship and institution of the creation as part of the revelation of what it means to be human. Each is important, each offers an opportunity for the exercise of human responsibility in relation to God.

Government's Responsibility for Human Development

One of the important nonfamilial institutions of human society that is essential to the communal life of the image of God is the political community—the institution constituted by citizens in relation to government. The task of discerning *what* government's responsibilities should be is part of the inescapable obligation humans have to respond to God's call to do justice to one another and to the whole creation. Because God alone is omnicompetent, we will look for the limited and particular responsibility that belongs to government and will recognize that government's responsibility to do justice to all requires that it protect the diverse nongovernment responsibilities of

citizens. A biblical point of view entails both a very high view of human beings as the image of God and the firm conviction that a wide variety of adult
responsibilities in a differentiated society is essential to the existence of a just
social order.

A properly ordered society is one in which government's basic function
is to uphold the multiple accountability structures of society. The kind of
"standard governmental operating policies" I have in mind may, for example, include the income tax deduction for dependents; public funding for
parentally chosen education; the fair and equitable enforcement of contracts; a social security system; health-care insurance; and enforceable rules
for public health and well-being, such as garbage disposal, fire protection,
and the swift and just punishment of criminal behavior. With regard to
these general functions of seeing to the just ordering of society, government
is fulfilling its responsibilities when it recognizes and supports individuals
and other institutions that have responsibilities for the rearing and educating of children, for the development and offering of jobs, for the provision
of health care, and so forth.

But there are also circumstances in which unusual, even catastrophic,
crises arise. These may be natural disasters, such as earthquakes, hurricanes,
or floods. They may come as a result of war, massive civil unrest, or a crime
wave. Under these circumstances, most of us have no difficulty in seeing
that the state is the legitimate authority to exercise emergency powers for
the protection of the public commonwealth. To the extent that poverty or
lack of health security for seniors appears to place the society in a critical
condition, then it may be time to ask whether the standard programs for
upholding the public welfare are sufficient to address the need. If crime,
large-scale unemployment, poverty, or the grave failure of schooling reveals
social degeneracy that cannot be overcome by means of standard public operating policies, then emergency powers may be needed to help reorder the
situation.

Obviously, an emergency response by government to deformities caused
by various human irresponsibilities is something quite different from flying in
massive supplies of food and water to hurricane victims. People enduring a
natural disaster are presumed to be capable of fulfilling ordinary responsibilities once they receive the emergency assistance. Within weeks or months,
the emergency operation can be called off. But in the case of a vast social/
cultural crisis in a differentiated society, it is precisely the density of crimi-
nals, or of illiterate and unemployed people, or of children without adequate
homes that creates the problem. The need is not simply for a few more food

stamps or new textbooks or better locks on the doors. The kind of emergency action needed in the case of cultural breakdown may require government's coordination, but clearly the means will have to be different from those used to address a large-scale natural disaster.

Beyond government's standard public operating policies and its preparedness to respond to emergencies, it should also seek to fulfill its calling by working diligently to reform fundamentally unjust structures in society. This is the level at which the most difficult judgments have to be made about public responsibility for social and economic well-being. The needs may be urgent, but remedies require long-term change. Better schools, better job training, more responsible parents, a decrease in crime, improved health care, better environmental protection, more extensive human support networks among families and across neighborhoods—all of these are needed in a differentiated society, but they cannot be created solely by government and shipped in from the outside.

Even here, however, if we begin with the idea that government's job is to support the recovery of diverse human responsibilities in a variety of institutions, seeing to it that justice is done to each of them, then some significant new pointers can be given to policymakers. Instead of trying directly to liberate individuals from bad circumstances by giving them public funds or other assistance, policymakers should look for ways to strengthen and assist parents, teachers, employers, and organizations such as churches and social-service organizations that are capable of offering meaningful, direct, personal assistance. Instead of looking only at measurements of economic inequality, policymakers will need to consider measurements of "responsibility inequality" to see how people can be encouraged (and in some cases compelled) to fulfill the responsibilities that are tied to the exercise of their adult freedom.

The argument of this chapter has been exploratory. It emphasizes the importance of the basic assumptions and presuppositions that guide human thinking about government's task in society. Radically different views of human nature often lead to radically different views of human purpose and responsibility. That is part of the reason for our current difficulty in developing sound social, educational, welfare, and health-care policies. Americans do not share a consensus about human identity and responsibility, including the responsibility of government, though too many still fall back on either a conservative or liberal version of classical liberalism.

A Christian worldview, fostering a Christian-democratic approach to politics and government, opens eyes to a creation filled with people created in the image of God, capable of being both responsible and irresponsible in a wide variety of ways. In God's creation, human beings play a creative role in shaping complex, differentiating societies as an expression of what it means to be human. In these complex social orders, government's task should be to uphold the justice of the public commons and to help strengthen the accountability structures in which people hold a diverse range of obligations to one another, to the rest of creation, and to God.

~

CHAPTER FOUR

E Pluribus Unum and Faith-Based Welfare Reform

Since 1996, when President Clinton signed into law a major reform of federal welfare programs, the debate about religion and government has taken a new turn. The primary reasons for this are the Charitable Choice provision in the welfare-reform law followed by President Bush's creation of a new White House Office of Faith-Based and Community Initiatives in 2001, designed to extend the implications of Charitable Choice.[1] In essence, Charitable Choice says that state governments, when cooperating with nongovernment social service organizations and using federal welfare funds, may no longer exclude religious service providers from cooperation with government due to their religious character. Nor may government demand of a religious service organization, as a condition for its cooperation, that it "secularize" its operations in order to hide or eliminate its religious character and motivation. Why has this relatively small ingredient in a massive welfare-reform policy caused such heated debate?

According to Larry Eichel, writing in the *Philadelphia Inquirer* (8 March 2001), it is because the issues involved go "right to the heart of what this nation is about." Indeed, I would contend that if the principles of Charitable Choice are implemented successfully and remain in place over time, the consequence will be a significant reordering of American pluralism, of *e pluribus unum*, with respect to both religion and the diverse institutions and organizations of society. The outcome could well be a *fourth order of pluralism* in the republic. For the controversy has everything to do with competing definitions of religion, with incompatible ideas of what defines the unity of a political community, and with different understandings of how the diverse associations and institutions of society are held together and protected in their own integrity. The controversy has to do precisely with the age-old questions of tolerance and intolerance, of exclusiveness and inclusiveness, of the relation of public religions to political authority.[2]

Historical Context

In order to understand the contemporary contention over government's relation to faith-based organizations, we need a brief sketch of the historical background. The *first order of pluralism*—as I am calling it—in the United States was established at the founding between 1776 and 1791. Before that time, the general pattern for a state or colony was some form of established or privileged religion, some kind of ecclesiastical or confessional prequalification for citizenship, thought to be necessary to hold the polity together. The bold move made by adding the Bill of Rights to the federal Constitution of 1787 was to declare that the new Congress would have no authority to legislate with respect to an establishment of religion or the inhibition of its free exercise. This first order of pluralism for the republic as a whole meant that each state was still free to make its own determination, without interference from Congress, about religious privilege and religious freedom. The national federation would be pluralistic, making room for a diversity of state religious establishments as each determined for itself.[3] This was not yet equal treatment for each American citizen as we have come to understand it today.

It is also important to emphasize that at the founding, state constitutions recognized as a condition for government (or took for granted in the common law) the rights of a variety of nongovernment institutions and associations, such as the family and the church, whose authority does not derive from government. In other words, each state's authority, as well as the federal government's authority, was constitutionally limited in competence, or, to state it negatively, was denied omnicompetence.

Now, as we know, the states either led or soon followed the federal government in disestablishing their churches, Massachusetts being the last to do so in the 1830s.[4] Those relatively quiet historical developments established what I would call the *second order of pluralism* in the United States. Each state, just like the federal government, accepted the principle that its unity—its *unum*—would be defined by something other than a common church or a congressionally authorized religion. The diversity of religions within each state would be given equal treatment. Part of what made this second order of pluralism possible was the fact that the country's population in the early nineteenth century shared a largely Christian/theistic/deistic heritage and climate of moral opinion, and many state constitutions and governments encouraged such a culture.

Note that this experiment in confessional pluralism did not aim to privatize religion. A diversity of churches, though not yet a wide range of religions, was recognized as having equal standing by virtue of the fact that none was established or given special public treatment. Yet this development occurred in large measure because a significant majority of the people shared a religiously grounded, publicly unifying ethos. Concern about how to keep the public moral cohesion strong was in fact the impetus for the establishment of common schools in the early nineteenth century, as advocated by Thomas Jefferson, Horace Mann, Benjamin Rush, and others. With a common ethos no longer guaranteed by an established church, some other means was thought to be necessary to assure that all Americans would be nurtured in a common public morality.[5] Yet, it was taken for granted that the public ethos—the common public morality—was religion friendly.

Part of the reason for the religious character of the republic, even after it had disestablished all churches, is that the Puritan ideal of establishing a "city on a hill"—a new covenant people of God—was attached to the country as a whole. The original Puritan ideal was ambiguous because the New England colonists had established a polity whose voting citizens had to be members of the Congregational Church. When too many citizens were no longer church members, the undifferentiated religious-political community could not survive. For many Christians thereafter, it was only the church that represented God's new covenant community. Yet as the colonies joined together to fight for their independence and then to form states and an independent federation, the myth of America as God's chosen nation was born. With the strong providential language of the Declaration of Independence, the founders created "a nation with the soul of a church," as G. K. Chesterton once said.

The critical moment that served to define the second order of pluralism for roughly the next one hundred years occurred when Catholics began to immigrate in large numbers into New York and Massachusetts in the early 1800s. The largely Protestant majority, which was learning to live *without* established churches but *with* various types of common schools that reflected their civil-religious idea of the nation, quickly reached the conclusion that there would be no room for Catholic schools in the public commons. Consequently, public school societies were established by the Protestant majority in New York and Boston to make sure that only "nonsectarian" schools would be recognized as common schools and supported with public funds. The Catholic schools were classified as "sectarian" and granted freedom of operation only in private, paid for privately, outside the bounds of the supposedly nonsectarian public commons.[6] Pluralism for schooling and moral education now meant essentially the same as pluralism for churches, namely, freedom for sectarian diversity in private. Public unity would be maintained by nurturing children in the moral ethos of the majority in the common schools, which were recognized as part of the public sphere. White Anglo-Saxon Protestants, though only a majority, thus claimed a monopoly over government-supported schooling. These now officially established schools came to serve some of the same purposes that established churches had served earlier. They provided the moral and religious training needed by youngsters who were expected to become God-fearing citizens in the new nation.

Keep in mind that in the mid-nineteenth-century, the word "nonsectarian" did not mean nonreligious or anti-religious. The common schools read the Bible, studied the Bible, said prayers, and inculcated a Protestant/theistic/deistic moral point of view. Thus, outside the churches, public religion flourished, but it was increasingly thought of as part of the nation's common moral ethos—and thus "nonsectarian"—over against Catholic "sectarianism." The word "sectarian" in this context was not primarily a reference to the Catholic church as a Christian sect, but to the Catholic community's position in the nonsectarian republic. The republic itself was taking on the character of a universal (nonsectarian) civil-religious community, and citizens could choose either to be full members in good standing and enjoy free education in the common schools or to live on the fringes as tolerated sectarians. Gradually, the WASP majority lost consciousness of the religious character of its public identity and common schools. The word "religion" increasingly came to be used to refer only to churches and sectarian practices that had to be kept in private because they had no place in the established republic.

What happened was that a very religious, cultural set of WASP beliefs established the public conditions for associational or institutional freedom and unqualified citizenship in the republic. Catholics were allowed to associate freely in exclusive churches, just as Protestants were. The United States could establish pluralism for a diversity of exclusive churches because the all-inclusive identity of the republic was not tied to any ecclesiastical entity. However, by contrast, education, though once conducted in diverse ways and in a variety of nongovernment schools, would henceforth be treated chiefly as a public, governmental establishment, and the unified republic, mirrored in each state, would be upheld by the common ethos inculcated in the common schools.

There was an inconsistency or unresolved dilemma here, however. If education is a department of state and if common schooling for every child is necessary to hold the society together, why did public officials allow some citizens to opt out of the common schools? On the other hand, since public officials did grant that many independent and "sectarian" schools could remain open, why did those officials not acknowledge the fact that schooling was not necessarily (and never had been merely) a department of state? Local and state governments have, indeed, set up schools, but schools have also been established by other institutions and associations as well. Moreover, the responsibility for raising and educating minor children was then, and continues to be, acknowledged in law as the responsibility of parents. Thus, in the educational arena a considerable ambiguity arose about the relation of government to nongovernment institutions.[7] The same ambiguity, we will see, later took hold in the welfare policy arena.

If, by the middle 1800s, most Catholics had chosen to send their children to the culturally Protestant ("nonsectarian") public schools, then the education of Catholic children would have been fully supported by public funding. Of course, the Catholics would have had to agree to submit their children to schooling that was, in many ways, non-Catholic. But to the extent that Catholics insisted on using their own schools, their educational efforts were denied equal public treatment because government defined Catholic schools as "sectarian." On these terms, you can see, there was no room for *public educational pluralism* in the United States. That which had become the informal religion of the republic was quite evident in the prayers and (King James) Bible readings of the publicly established schools, but since these schools were run by states and local communities, not by churches, their religious character gradually receded from view.

The *third order of pluralism* took hold in the United States as the result of the further secularization of the second order and became dominant by the middle of the twentieth century. This is the pluralist order most familiar to us today. It is taken for granted in the constitutional arguments made by today's ACLU, Americans United for the Separation of Church and State, and People for the American Way. I would even venture to say that it is the framework now taken for granted by most Christians, both Protestant and Catholic, and Jews. To identify this third order, we need only look at how the words "nonsectarian" and "sectarian" are used, quite in contrast to the way they were used in the nineteenth century. The word "nonsectarian" now means "secular" or "nonreligious" and no longer corresponds to the ethos of older cultural Protestantism. The word "sectarian" now refers not only to "Catholics," but to all who are explicitly or self-professedly "religious." The underlying political structure has not changed: the supposedly nonsectarian political majority still claims the right to monopolize the public square while upholding pluralism in private for "sectarians." But the change in the connotation and denotation of the terms reflects a significantly new meaning of pluralism.

To say this is not to imply that an American civil religion has disappeared, but only that its character is now more deistic and secularized, framed more by an Enlightenment point of view than by the older Protestant consensus. Also keep in mind that it is during the time when this third order of pluralism came to dominate public opinion and the courts that the largest and greatest number of public welfare programs was established. By definition, the major federal programs to end or alleviate poverty, joblessness, drug abuse, and other poverty-inducing or poverty-aggravating problems were put forward as *secular* public programs, programs of and by government for citizens identified in their "secular" capacity. Almost all discussion of poverty and welfare since the 1960s has focused on government's actions toward secular citizens, with the consequence that most nongovernment programs of poverty relief fell from public view, despite the fact that those nongovernment services have made a huge public difference.[8] The same pattern holds in the educational arena. Public discussion of education policy and funding focuses almost entirely on "public" schools even though 12–18 percent of American children receive their publicly approved education in independent schools or at home.

Under the third pluralistic regime, one can understand why government aid to anything identified as sectarian—now including more than Catholics schools—had to be declared out of bounds. Ellen Willis makes the following profession of faith:

> I believe that a democratic polity requires a secular state: one that does not fund or otherwise sponsor religious institutions and activities; that does not display religious symbols; that outlaws discrimination based on religious belief, whether by government or by private employers, landlords or proprietors— that does, in short, guarantee freedom from as well as freedom of religion. Furthermore, a genuinely democratic society requires a secular ethos: one that does not equate morality with religion, stigmatize atheists, defer to religious interests and aims over others or make religious belief an informal qualification for public office. Of course, secularism in the latter sense is not mandated by the First Amendment. It's a matter of sensibility, not law.[9]

What makes Willis's language work is the unquestioned assumption that there is nothing religious or confessional about her own profession of faith. The language used counts on the reader agreeing that religion is a separable, private matter. However, if one recognizes this profession of secular faith for the faith that it is, just as one can now recognize the religious character of the nineteenth-century majority's profession of "nonsectarianism," then Willis's words have to be reinterpreted in order to be fair and nonimpositional toward people of other faiths.[10] In such a turnabout Willis would have to contend that the state should not "sponsor religious—including secularist—institutions and activities; that it not display religious—including secularist—symbols; that it outlaw discrimination based on religious—including secularist—belief . . . ; that, in short, it guarantee freedom from as well as freedom of religion—including secularism." A "genuinely democratic society" should, in other words, require a genuinely neutral ethos.[11] Such an argument points us toward the fourth order of pluralism to which I will turn in a moment, but first we must say something more about the third order of pluralism.

In a system where pluralism is assured to "sectarians" only in private, the only way an explicitly religious organization can participate in a publicly funded program is by demonstrating its willingness to function in public in a "nonsectarian" fashion. Catholic Charities, for example, has been free to serve as an extension of government's social service deliveries as long as it has agreed to act in a secular manner, which no one would mistakenly identify as Catholic.[12] These are also the terms on which Catholic schools have been able to win small amounts of public funding for *secular* aspects of schooling, such as busing, lunches, and certain textbooks. Secularizing the "nonsectarian" public square has also required the removal of prayer and Bible reading from the government-funded schools. Quite evidently, then, the third order of pluralism represents a new version of moral majoritarianism. The moral requirements for public inclusion—for equal public participation—have become those of the secular majority, no longer of the Protestant majority, and all professedly religious and sectarian moral convictions must be held and exercised privately.

The odd thing here is the way that this ideological point of view has been absorbed voluntarily by nongovernment organizations. Independent, often explicitly religious entities, have taken the reigning dualism into themselves, into their very identities. Whether as schools or as social-service organizations, they have agreed to identify their confessional commitment as a purely private matter. Agreeing to cooperate with government and its public funding then means agreeing to redefine part of themselves as an extension of the secular public. As America's religious and moral diversity kept expanding during the twentieth century, and as the number and kinds of nongovernment organizations continued to expand, room was made for everyone as long as everyone agreed to keep their sectarian differences outside public institutions and to conform to the secular norms of the majority in public life.

This frame of mind is evident in the writings of Amy Gutman, Dennis Thompson, James Bohman, Stephen Macedo, John Rawls, and others who say that America needs to strengthen "deliberative democracy" in the face of our growing multiculturalism. However, as Ashley Woodiwiss, quoting Chantal Mouffe, explains in a recent review article, "the proponents of deliberative democracy 'generally start by stressing what they call the "fact of pluralism" and then proceed to find procedures to deal with differences whose objective is actually to make those differences irrelevant and to relegate pluralism to the sphere of the private.'"[13] This is pluralism of the third order.

Challenges to the "Secularized" Public Square

A major public challenge to the deepening secularization of the American public square was mounted by groups such as the Moral Majority, beginning in the 1970s. These groups still breathe the air of the moral/religious ethos of second-order pluralism. Jerry Falwell, Pat Robertson, and others cannot accept that the old public consensus has dissolved, so they assume that a secular minority has illegitimately seized the monopoly privilege of the majority. The so-called New Religious Right wanted, and for the most part continues to want, to uphold pluralism in private for sectarian faiths, including freedom for atheists and secularists, but they do not want a minority secularist ethos to control the public square. They are not trying to recover the first order of pluralism, in which each state had the right to establish Christianity, and even a particular church. Charges of this sort against the Moral Majority, the Christian Coalition, and Focus on the Family by third-order pluralists are mistaken and are intended to frighten ordinary citizens. No, the resurgent conservatives simply want to reestablish the pre-secularized, nineteenth-century moral order in which the word "nonsectarian" referred to the WASP consensus that once served as the civil-religious glue of the country. For second-order pluralists the protection of religion in private goes hand in hand with public rule by those who have the same moral sensibilities as those who go to church and acknowledge God.

By contrast, for third-order pluralists the guarantee of religious freedom goes hand in hand with public secularity. The only legitimate moral major-

ity today, in their view, is the one that works vigorously to exclude all sectarian preferences, languages, and doctrines other than its own from control
of the public square. Religion, they insist, is a private matter that should be
disconnected from, and left unaided by, government. The non-establishment
of religion means no entanglement with sectarian activities; the free exercise
of religion means freedom in private to be as sectarian as one chooses. A secular view of public life, even if held only by a majority, should, on these
terms, monopolize schooling and welfare services. But of course, People for
the American Way is no less sectarian in the eyes of the Christian Coalition
than is the Moral Majority in the eyes of Americans United for the Separation of Church and State.

One can see from this simple sketch why at one level in today's contention over the new faith-based initiatives the conflict truly is all-or-
nothing, because each claimant to public moral authority and political power
wants to monopolize the entire public square. The structure of the conflict is
the same for Pat Robertson and Barry Lynn, the director of Americans
United. Both want the majority to hold a monopoly in the public square with
the right to determine who and what is sectarian. But whereas Robertson is
a second-order pluralist who is willing to let secularists thrive in private
where they cannot, for example, write the curricula for public school class-
rooms, Lynn wants a secular majority to control school curricula and define
the terms of publicly funded welfare services while making room for Falwell
and other fundamentalist sectarians in private quarters alone. The battle is
all or nothing—a true culture war—because neither viewpoint can envision
genuine *public* pluralism. The side that gains control of Congress, the courts,
and the schools, will claim the right to define what the entire nonsectarian
republic should be.

However, as much as the media prefer a simple two-sided conflict, the
contention over Charitable Choice and faith-based social policy today is actually three-sided, not two-sided. The reason is that a new and different view
of pluralism has joined the fray, presenting a challenge to both second-order
and third-order pluralists. The new pluralist challenge also emerged in the
1970s and 1980s and is an ingredient in both the Charitable Choice provision as well as the White House Office on Faith-Based and Community Initiatives. For this reason, the true significance of Charitable Choice cannot be
grasped within the framework in which it is being contested by second- and
third-order pluralists, the framework that most commentators and the media
take for granted.

Peter Dobkin Hall, for example, contends that "the concerns expressed a
century ago" about government's subsidizing of "sectarian institutions" differ

little from those expressed in our contemporary debate. "The main difference," he says, "was that [in the late 1800s] most Protestants (especially evangelicals) opposed government subsidy because they felt that most of the money went to Catholics."[14] While it is true, as we've said, that the framework in which a "nonsectarian" majority worries about funding "sectarians" remained the same from the nineteenth century through the twentieth, Hall overlooks the significant change in the meaning of the words "nonsectarian" and "sectarian" from the 1840s to the 1940s and thus misses the important cultural shift that took place. Moreover, Hall does not see the even greater difference between the public monopoly claims voiced by both the nineteenth- and the twentieth-century majoritarians, on the one hand, and the new pluralist framework that undergirds Charitable Choice, on the other. There are, in fact, important differences among the three contenders in today's debate.

A New Pluralism

In contrast to the first three orders of pluralism in the United States, *the fourth order of pluralism* for which I am contending requires a different understanding of religion, political order, and social diversity.[15] The new pluralism starts with the understanding that the religions by which people live, whether traditional or modern, whether acknowledged or unacknowledged, exert themselves in public life and not only in private quarters. The effort to force a private, "sectarian" confinement on religious ways of life is itself a form of religious imperialism. The Enlightenment's dichotomy of a secular public on the one hand and religious privacy on the other arises from a religiously deep and all-encompassing worldview. It is no more neutral or tolerant or all-inclusive than was the nineteenth century's Protestant cultural ethos. The Latin word "*saeculum*" means "of or pertaining to this age," or to this world. Until the modern era, it was taken for granted that "this world"— the secular—is connected to and dependent on God. It is true that the words "religion" and "religious" came to be associated with the Catholic Church's authority structure, church vocations, orders, worship, and the Eucharist. Even after the Protestant Reformation reaffirmed the priesthood of all believers and the importance of recognizing "vocations" in all areas of life as religious service to God, the words "religion" and "religious" continued to be used mostly to refer to church-related activities of worship, piety, and evangelism. Nevertheless, there is no basis in those traditions, or in Judaism or Islam, for thinking of the "secular" as unrelated to God or of the "religious" as belonging to the church alone or to inner personal space alone. The modern presumption that the "secular" world stands on its own, dependent on nothing beyond itself, represents a radical change in worldviews, a fundamental religious reorientation or conversion, a basic change in assumptions. There is nothing religiously neutral about a view of reality that insists on privatizing the religious and disconnecting it from a supposedly religion-free *saeculum*. Thus, from the new pluralist point of view, it is not possible to speak of the "religious" and the "secular" in modern, Enlightenment terms.

If we now reread the Constitution's First Amendment from the viewpoint of fourth-order pluralism, the religion clauses appear in a different light. The First Amendment does not call for public secularity and the privatization of religion. It does not grant to a religious majority, disguised as a nonsectarian guardian of the public square, the right to define certain confessional viewpoints as sectarian and thus ineligible for equal treatment by government. Instead, the First Amendment says that religious free exercise really must be protected in public as well as in private life and that the establishment of religion can only be avoided by treating all citizens equally and not granting the privilege of establishment to any religion or ideology. The First Amendment's non-establishment clause does not mean "no aid to religious groups"; it means no establishment of any religion or religiously equivalent worldview. If the convictions of citizens, whether Christian or secularist, whether Jewish or Muslim, guide them to serve their neighbors with drug treatment and job training programs, then government may not discriminate against any of them when it invites nongovernment organizations to cooperate with it in serving those who need drug treatment and job training.

What about Jerry Falwell's and Pat Robertson's worry that such an open and nondiscriminatory pluralism may mean government's support of what they consider to be objectionable sects? That is a worry that only makes sense from the point of view of a second- or third-order pluralist who presumes that the country's majority should have the political authority to decide what is an objectionable religion. In the nineteenth century, it was Catholics and then Mormons who were considered to be the objectionable and dangerous sects. For third-order pluralists, the Christian Coalition is as objectionable as scientologists and black Muslims; they are all sectarians. For the new pluralism, by contrast, the principle that should hold is equal public treatment of all faiths, with none having the right, through control of government, to monopolize public policy and funding for its point of view.

This takes us to the heart of the matter regarding government's cooperation with faith-based social-service ministries and organizations. Today's secularized nonsectarians define all public welfare and social programs not only as secular but as *governmental* through and through. The implication is that anything government touches or funds, any organization it works with in social-service or education delivery, must be treated as an extension of government and its purposes. Moreover, if government and its services have already been defined as secular, then ipso facto, any organization with which government chooses to cooperate becomes a secular extension of government. In this case, not only does the secular triumph over the religious, but government overwhelms the nongovernmental.

There are two mistakes in this way of thinking and policy making. First, as we've already argued, government has no constitutional right to define its terrain as "secular" and to outlaw religion from public expression. That is a discriminatory imposition of secular sectarianism. Second, government ought not to obliterate or undermine that which is legitimately nongovernmental—the families, churches, business enterprises, and diverse nongovernment associations organized outside of government. Whenever government cooperates with nongovernment organizations, it has every obligation to recognize and protect the independent integrity of those organizations, including their confessional freedom. The relationship should be one of partnership, not co-optation and takeover. There are countless examples at local, state, and federal levels where government cooperates, whether by contract or by some other means, with organizations that have their own reason for being and for serving people.

Consider, for example, one of the most obvious religious partnerships of the federal government, namely the military chaplaincy. The military services pay the salaries and provide the commissions, uniforms, and offices for those who also, at the same time, serve as ordained clergy of their respective religious bodies. We do not presume for a moment that because the government employs and pays for the chaplains it thereby has the right to take over or incorporate the institutions that those chaplains represent. Nor do the chaplains then become a simple extension of government. The chaplaincy program gives the government no authority to require the Catholic Church to ordain women or to demand that Muslims be nondiscriminatory in their hiring practices by hiring Baptist or Presbyterian chaplains. No, the relationship is a partnership in which government and religious institutions cooperate, each fulfilling its own purpose. The integrity of each is upheld. Government does not *do* priestly and pastoral work, but it can cooperate with organizations that do.

Ambiguity has arisen in the areas of education and welfare policy because in both of these areas government has presumed to *do* education and poverty relief. One answer to this ambiguity could be offered by arguing that government ought not to set up schools and welfare agencies as a direct extension of government. Instead, it ought to partner with independent schools and agencies, providing funding and other means in an equitable, pluralist manner. Another answer is that even when government sets up its own schools and welfare agencies, it should give them no advantage or privilege that is denied to independent schools and service organizations. Thus, when government acts on its obligation to provide for the public welfare by determining that a certain class or sector of eligible citizens should receive certain services, it ought to proceed in a way that takes fully into account the organizations that are already offering such services. If it chooses to partner with such organizations, it can do justice to them and to all eligible recipients only by preserving the full integrity of all parties. Government must establish its own general qualifications, conditions, and purposes for the service it mandates or funds, but justice also requires that it not discriminate against any qualified nongovernment organization because it is religious or nongovernmental. The question of an organization's secular or nonsecular viewpoint is simply irrelevant. The proper question from government's side is whether the organizations that agree to cooperate with it can demonstrate a capability of serving those who are eligible for the service.[16] And this is where confessional pluralism is so important. Not every group will be able to serve every eligible person, nor will every eligible person want to receive his or her benefits indiscriminately from every service provider. The government's general or universal public purpose can best be fulfilled through partnership with a diversity of providers that can, in a variety of ways and from a variety of viewpoints, reach all the different kinds of eligible recipients.

Look again, by analogy, at the military chaplaincy program. Government's general public service is to provide military chaplains. Recognizing that military personnel require chaplains of different confessions, the government partners with diverse religious institutions to recruit a diverse range of chaplains in proportion to the need for them. Government does not first create a uniform public profession of faith and way of worship and then demand that, regardless of the chaplain's religion of origin, he or she put "sectarian" commitments aside and become a "nonsectarian" chaplain for everyone. What the military actually does is to demonstrate the principle that should hold true for social and welfare services. A wide variety of groups in the United States may offer drug treatment, job training, and other services in different ways and from different points of view. As long as eligible recipients are free to enter and exit the programs, and as long as no service organization has a monopoly in a territory, then government properly fulfills its general obligation by partnering with a diversity of demonstrably capable service organizations without regard to the viewpoints, philosophies, and religions of the latter.

The new pluralism directly challenges the argument by third-order plural-ists that faith-based organizations which receive public funds should not be al-lowed to discriminate in their hiring practices. Rep. Bobby Scott (D-VA) and Barry Lynn say that an independent service-provider's right to hire in accor-dance with its convictions "would allow religious bigotry in hiring to be prac-ticed with the use of federal funds."[17] The error here begins with the denial that any true partnership can exist because every participating organization be-comes, by definition, an extension of government. Thus, any group that serves the needy represents the single public monopoly that stands behind those funds. On Scott and Lynn's terms, any discrimination in hiring is the same as public exclusion based on bigotry. But that is nonsense from a genuinely plu-ralist point of view. There is absolutely no discrimination being practiced by a Pentecostal drug-rehabilitation center when it hires a person of Pentecostal faith qualified to perform the service and refuses to hire an atheist or a Muslim, as long as atheist and Muslim drug-rehabilitation centers are free to hire whomever they want for the programs they operate. Catholic chaplains or-dained exclusively by the Catholic Church are not keeping Jewish chaplains from serving those who want a Jewish chaplain, as long as the government that employs the chaplains remains fully pluralistic in its partnerships.

The second error in the Scott/Lynn argument is the presumption that the religious or ideological commitment of the people who provide welfare ser-vices is irrelevant to the "secular" service being provided. The fact is that the food, or shelter, or job training, or drug treatment being offered by many groups is offered as an act of Christian, or Muslim, or humanist charity. In which case, the hiring of staff members who share a common motivation and commitment may be integral to the job's definition, just as Catholic, or Jew-ish, or Lutheran faith is integral to the job of a military chaplain. Govern-ment's nondiscriminatory, general public purpose is fulfilled precisely and only by not discriminating against any group, regardless of its religious point of view, when it decides to partner with any of them. The public delivery plan is pluralistic from the start so that no one is excluded. It is the Scott/Lynn argument that represents bigotry and illegitimate exclusiveness, because their prejudgment that government should exclude explicitly reli-gious groups from partnership with government altogether represents unjust religious discrimination from the outset. What Americans United and Peo-ple for the American Way cannot see is the anti-pluralist bias of their own argument and that is because the injustice resides in their most fundamental, unquestioned assumptions.

Charitable Choice does not call for special privileges for religious groups or a special pot of money exclusively for faith-based organizations; it simply requires the halt to public discrimination against such groups. That, of course, amounts to the end of public-monopoly privileges for "secular" moral majoritarians as well as for "religious" moral majoritarians. A new order of pluralism will mean that all of America's communities will have the same legal protection to practice their religions and nonreligions freely in public and that they may do so in partnership with government in many instances. Religious freedom will no longer need to be conceived as a right that is protected only when completely disassociated from government. And this means that public Christians, along with people of every other religion, can be forthright in public life and live out their deepest convictions in the social and educational service they offer because they will be acting in accord with pluralist principles that assure the same freedom to every other group. Not only should citizens be free to worship or not worship in accord with their conscience, they should also be free to live their religions openly in public without discrimination and without opportunity to monopolize the public order for themselves. This is genuine pluralism. It is the only way to do justice to human beings who are at root religious creatures. This is what Christian-democratic political service is all about.

What about the worries of some religious and libertarian groups that "mixing government and charity . . . could undermine the very things that have made private charity so effective," and that "faith-based charities could find their missions shifting, their religious character lost, the very things that made them so successful destroyed," as Michael Tanner puts it?[18] First, if one presumes that whatever government touches it corrupts, then Tanner's argument holds. Further, if one assumes that no form of partnership can possibly preserve the integrity of the nongovernment organization, the argument also holds. And finally, if one presumes that faith-based efforts are, by definition, private and authentic only if they remain disconnected from government, then the argument holds.

The argument for a new pluralism, however, challenges all of these assumptions. Neither second-order nor third-order pluralism can do justice to contemporary reality and public welfare policy. The argument of Ellen Willis is the flip side of Michael Tanner's. Both make the same assumption about a dominating, demanding, secular government that leaves nothing that it touches unsecularized. And both make the same assumption that religion and charity belong in private. From the viewpoint of the new pluralism, any group or religion that conceives of itself and its purpose as entirely private should, of course, be free not to partner with government. There is nothing about Charitable Choice that says all religious social-service organizations *must* partner with government. At the same time, the government's aim should be to define the nature of its partnerships so that every religious organization, just as every cooperating organization that thinks of itself as not religious, will be fully free and responsible to maintain its own integrity and mission.

This is the context in which the new pluralism rejects the whole idea that cooperation between government and faith-based groups requires a prior determination to segregate the public's "secular" funds and services from the "sectarian" elements of the faith-based groups that cooperate in providing the service. The mistaken assumption of third-order pluralists continues to be that the "nonsectarian" secular function (which belongs in the public domain) is a religion-free zone and must be separated from the "sectarian" function or domain in any organization that chooses to partner with government. But, according to the Constitution's First Amendment, the privilege of constructing this dichotomy does not belong to government, for it does not lie in government's authority to define, prescribe, or proscribe the nature of religion.[19] There may indeed be groups like Catholic Charities that think of themselves as a two-part composite of the secular and the religious. There may be other groups that think of themselves as integrally religious or as integrally secular. None of this need concern government. Its only concern, when cooperating with nongovernment organizations, should be to make sure that the partnering organizations demonstrate the ability to perform or provide the service. If an organization is proving that it can help drug addicts break their habits and if that is government's general public purpose in funding drug-rehabilitation services, then the philosophy or religious orientation of different nongovernment organizations is of no concern to government, as long as those eligible to receive the services are free to choose or not choose, to enter and exit, the various programs.

One way to avoid potential entanglement problems for government is for it to fund vouchers for eligible recipients so they can choose a service provider. For various government programs, from food supplements to child care to drug rehabilitation, vouchers might, indeed, be the best and most efficient means of providing funding to eligible individuals. However, from the new pluralist point of view, vouchers are not required for reasons that are peculiarly *religious*. If no group or majority is allowed to predefine the public's services as nonsectarian and thus to exclude "sectarians," then there will be no reason to give special attention to those unjustly excluded by giving vouchers for use in "sectarian" institutions. From the third-order pluralist point of view, vouchers may give the appearance of allowing individuals to make a "sectarian" choice without government being responsible for endorsing it. But government must still decide which organizations are allowed to accept and cash in the vouchers. One way or another, a counter-argument will be made either that "sectarian" organizations may not participate or that they must separate their "sectarian" part from their "nonsectarian" part in order to receive public funds for the "nonsectarian" service they offer. That entire framework must be dissolved if justice is to be done to all citizens and to all nongovernment organizations.

If the fourth order of pluralism takes hold and endures, then there will come a day when the words "nonsectarian" and "sectarian" will become as useless and obnoxious as the disparaging words that white Protestants once used to put down blacks and Catholics.[20] No one will then be able to get away with calling the public square secular, for it will finally be open to all faiths and ideologies, without an establishment or a privileged role for any of them. The new order will, for the first time, establish public and not just private pluralism and will eliminate monopoly privileges in the public square for any religious or ideological viewpoint.

CHAPTER FIVE

The Cause of Racial Justice

"The Supreme Court decision [*Brown v. Board of Education*] is the greatest victory for the Negro people since the Emancipation Proclamation," announced Harlem's *Amsterdam News* in 1954.[1] This year we celebrate the fiftieth anniversary of that landmark decision, which struck down laws that forced the segregation of whites and blacks in public schooling. The injustice of state-sponsored racial segregation appears all too obvious to almost everyone today. Yet, why did it take almost a hundred years after the Civil War to arrive at the *Brown* decision? And why is that decision still controversial today as the country and the court continue to struggle with the consequences of slavery and racial discrimination in American society? Although there is no legally enforced segregation in government-sponsored schools today, all schools are not equal, and the outcomes of education are not equal. Moreover, compared to fifty years ago, there is much greater racial diversity in the United States now, particularly with the growth of Latino and Asian populations. Where are we then in America today with respect to the cause of racial justice and the equal treatment of all citizens?

First, a word about terms. When I speak of "racism," I am referring to attitudes, habits, and institutional practices that manifest a deep bias against people of another race *because* of their race. I mean by racism a bias deep enough to constitute a conviction or enduring feeling that people of another race are of a lower human value and may deserve disadvantaged treatment. By "legalized racism" I mean public laws that represent and uphold racism as defined above. Legalized racism amounts to legally approved discrimination against citizens of one or more races. When legalized racism has been overturned and laws have been changed to uphold equal treatment of all citizens, then companies, organizations, or individuals who violate those civil rights laws may be challenged in the courts on the grounds of the nonracist standards of the law. While legalized racism has, for the most part, been eliminated in the United States, many practices continue to be contested in the courts, and many private attitudes, habits, and practices of a racist character remain.

Just and Unjust Discrimination

The verb "to discriminate" typically carries a negative connotation when used in the context of racism, although it means something very positive when used to refer to someone with "discriminating taste." With respect to racism it is important to understand the negative meaning of the word against the backdrop of its positive meaning. Someone who fails to distinguish or discriminate between a rose and an orchid, or between a school and a bank, or between a movie theater and a church, is making a mistake. To be able to discriminate properly between two different kinds of things is a positive virtue. How then have we come to use the word "discrimination" to mean a mistaken and morally negative act? The grave injustice of slavery and forced segregation were due precisely to a discriminating judgment that was wrong, to a distinction that was mistaken and *should never have been made.* The essential evil of slavery was that certain human beings, because of their color and place of origin, were identified as eligible to be bought and sold and owned by other humans as if they were property. Justice can only be done to humans, however, if all of them are recognized as human and none are mistakenly identified as property or as less valuable humans. The end of slavery and of forced segregation thereby demanded the *equal treatment* of all human beings before the law, *without discrimination.* In other words, if skin color provides no basis for legitimate legal discrimination among humans, and if all humans have the same identity as God's image, then all humans should be treated equally before the law.

While this may seem too obvious to emphasize, it is crucial because there are many dimensions of human life and many different kinds of responsibility that must be carefully distinguished if justice is to be done to humans in their full complexity. If, for example, we do not discriminate between children and adults when it comes to defining the labor market, we may allow youngsters to work in sweat shops and not get the education they need in order to mature. If we do not discriminate between profit-making and nonprofit corporations, we will miss something important. If we do not discriminate among schools and banks and families and churches, then the law cannot do justice to the distinctive character of each one. The first responsibility of all lawmaking and adjudication is to identify things properly—to discriminate rightly among different things—so that each can be given its due, so that justice can be done to each one. To discriminate where there is no basis for discrimination is unjust, but likewise, to fail to discriminate between different things is also to commit an injustice.

In the last fifty years, American law has rightly been trying to overcome unjust legal discrimination based on skin color, but in so doing, I want to argue, it has overlooked some important differences among spheres of human responsibility that require careful discrimination if justice is to be done to people of all races in the full complexity of their lives. One consequence is that some of the attempts to remedy racism have actually led to the unjust treatment of African Americans, among others. There can be no doubt that legalized racism based on a mistaken discrimination has been a universal blight on American society, traumatically affecting every sphere of life for African Americans. It is a sin of many generations that can never be adequately remedied. It must be repented of personally and by institutional means, including the replacement of unjust laws with just laws. Something that is not fundamental to human identity, namely skin color and land of origin, was used by slave-owning societies as the most fundamental and reductionistic identifier of black people who were then bought and sold with the full backing of the law. Black people were reduced to something less than human.

However, once legalized racism was reversed, subsequent legislation aiming to overcome educational, economic, and other disadvantages suffered by African Americans had to deal with the full complexity of life in American society, including the educational, economic, voluntary, and religious institutions involved. Once the universal, reductionistic identification that justified racial discrimination was no longer legal, the multidimensional character of social, economic, cultural, and political advancement of African Americans could no longer be addressed by the means used to oppose slavery and segregation.[2] Different kinds of social, economic, cultural, and political institutions had to be considered on their own terms, in their own integrity, with their own evaluative criteria. Not every inequality or injustice in every sphere of life can be traced to a racist origin, even though the long shadow of slavery and racial discrimination still hangs over us and impacts our lives.[3]

Consider the following analogy. Worldwide anti-colonial movements that achieved success during and after World War II showed considerable unity across a wide range of different colonial contexts. Large majorities of people in colonized areas rallied around those who led the fight against the single evil that affected all of colonial life. Once independence came, however, the focus on reconstruction and the governance of society had to discriminate carefully among differentiated institutions and responsibilities. Decisions about economic development, education, trade, the mutual accommodation of diverse racial, religious, and cultural groups all required different types of judgment appropriate to each sphere of life. For many countries at this stage, society-wide unity could not be achieved because different groups, different professions, and different economic interests disagreed about the terms of the public-legal unity that should organize their diverse responsibilities and ways of life. Cooperation could no longer be reduced to the single, simple common ground of fighting colonialism, even though the shadow of colonialism would hang over those countries for a long time to come.

Once the American civil rights movement had succeeded in changing the law so that it no longer discriminated against blacks because of their skin color, the positive construction and reconstruction of society required diverse judgments and discriminating strategies about economic, educational, cultural, and political reforms. It is not altogether surprising, then, that a coalition of many groups, religious and nonreligious, organized to oppose the one great evil of legalized racism, would have difficulty hanging together to promote five or ten great goods, each requiring different criteria of judgment about how to advance in each sphere. While it is true that all blacks suffered in many areas of life under legalized slavery and forced segregation, just as all former colonials suffered in many areas of life under colonial rule, the achievement of civil rights reform, like the overthrow of colonialism, presented the liberated ones with the possibility of exercising full, complex, diversified personhood in many human relationships and institutions. In other words, human identity could no longer be reduced to "black" or "colonial" as had been the case under oppression, but now had to become as fully differentiated as true human identity requires.

The Image of God

From a biblical point of view, human beings have their identity as the image of God. This means, among other things, that human identity cannot be reduced to one feature of the person or function of the society. As Kiini Ibura Salaam, a contemporary writer with a multicultural background, explains: "After walking between varying racial identifications, I know that race is no bastion of truth. . . . The biggest truth that race keeps at bay is that all of us are human."[4] Kimberly Springer from a mixed race family, and also a writer, comes at the same point in this intimate way: "The way that I communicate with my mother when we are having our ritual mother/daughter talk is certainly not 'white.' But, it's not 'black' either. Instead, it is woman-to-woman, love-to-love."[5]

Yet, if the image of God is not reducible to a racial identity, and if most Americans before the Civil War shared something of a biblical view of human identity, how do we account for the strong support of slavery among American Christians who claimed the authority of the Bible for their stance? How do we account for the contradiction that both supporters and opponents of slavery quoted the same Bible? As David Brion Davis explains, Christianity, along with most of the world's religions,

> had long given slavery its ultimate sanction. Catholic popes enthusiastically blessed and authorized the first Portuguese slave traders in West Africa. . . . In eighteenth-century Barbados the Church of England acquired possession of hundreds of slaves whose chests were branded with the letters "SOCIETY" to signify ownership by the Society for the Propagation of the Gospel. As late as the 1750s many devout British and American Quakers were actively involved in the slave trade.[6]

As Davis recounts the history, Lutherans, Huguenots, Calvinists, along with Muslims and Jews, all took up slavery as they gained access "to the immense profits generated from the world's first system of multinational production for a mass market—production of sugar, tobacco, coffee, chocolate, rum, dyestuffs, rice, spices, hemp, and cotton."[7]

How can we account for this? We can do so only by reiterating what we said in chapter 1, namely, that what Christians did was sinful and unjust and must now be judged not "Christian" in the sense that chattel slavery did not conform to the normative calling of God in Christ to do justice to all our neighbors. The "Christian" tradition of slavery was wrong. As Frederick Douglass put it in one of his great oratorical flourishes:

> What I have said respecting and against religion, I mean strictly to apply to the *slave-holding religion* of this land, and with no possible reference to Christianity proper; for, between the Christianity of this land, and the Christianity of Christ, I recognize the widest possible difference—so wide, that to receive the one as good, pure, and holy, is of necessity to reject the other as bad, corrupt, and wicked. To be the friend of the one, is of necessity to be the enemy of the other. I love the pure, peaceable, and impartial Christianity of Christ: I therefore hate the corrupt, slaveholding, women-whipping, cradle-plundering, par-

tial and hypocritical Christianity of this land. . . . We have men-stealers for ministers, women-whippers for missionaries, and cradle-plunderers for church members. . . . We have men sold to build churches, women sold to support the gospel, and babes sold to purchase Bibles for the *poor heathen! all for the glory of God and the good of souls!*[8]

Christian opposition to "Christian" slavery is evident, says Davis, in the fact that when late in the eighteenth century sustained protests against slavery finally began to pick up steam, "the Anglo-American antislavery movements were overwhelmingly religious in character, and drew on developments in sectarian and evangelical Protestantism."[9] In other words, the very Bible on which slave owners and traders depended to justify slavery provided both fuel and criteria for the abolition movement. The Bible accounts for sin and disobedience against God, including the misuse and mistreatment of humans by humans. American slaves found in the Exodus story and in Jesus the hope and motivation for their release from bondage. They and many who were not enslaved—like William Wilberforce—were gripped by the gospel to fight for the end of the wicked institution. This is one reason why the distinction between biblical norm and Christian practice is so important. Normative standards of justice, love, and good stewardship should not be identified with what Christians have done, because at each step along the way, behavior patterns have to be subjected to God's critical standards. This is as old as the blessings and cursings that God promised Israel after liberation from Egypt. Christian criticism of slavery and forced segregation is rooted in the biblical prophetic tradition. But why did it take so long to end slavery and to reach the civil rights reforms of the 1950s and 1960s? To understand this we need to grasp the limits of the liberal tradition, of our federal system, and of the American civil religion.

Different Expectations

What was the American public's understanding of the civil rights movement as it emerged in the 1950s and 1960s? On what terms did the majority, including Christians of various stripes, promote or at least acquiesce in the rejection of legal discrimination—legalized racism—against African Americans? What were their expectations of the consequences? While it would be impossible to know for sure the answers to these questions, I want to offer a generalization with two aims in mind. The first aim is to contrast white public opinion generally with the opinion of most African Americans and civil rights leaders—both black and white—whether religiously motivated or not.

The second aim is to use this contrast to shed light on the roots of current differences of opinion regarding further attempts to end racial discrimination.

With regard to public opinion over the past fifty years, white Americans have by now largely accepted civil rights advances for a variety of reasons. First, against the backdrop of the constitutional amendments that followed the North's victory in the Civil War and in the face of post-World War II court rulings and federal legislation, even those who did not applaud the civil rights movement were inclined to abide by the law once the reforms were in place. They were followers, not leaders. Second, many were moved by the nonviolent protests under the leadership of Martin Luther King Jr., which made manifest to a national public the unjust, unconstitutional treatment of African Americans. As a consequence, many were moved for moral reasons to accept changes in the law that overcame legalized racial discrimination. Finally, most Americans came to accept for blacks what they already took for granted for themselves, namely, the promise that hard work would provide the opportunity for every immigrant or naturally born American to make one's way in American society on the same terms as everyone else.

In stating the generality this way, two qualifications are important. First, I believe that a large percentage of Americans, and not only southerners, remained uncomfortable about the fact that the courts and the federal government had to impose changes of this magnitude. Their discomfort was due to the fact that social life and social policy outside the South between the Civil War and the Great Depression had, over time, changed primarily through the impact of social and economic developments under conditions of local and state governance rather than by federal mandate. Suspicion of the federal government has its roots in the American founding and was basic to American ideology generally and not only in the South. Similar reservations about federally imposed change had been expressed in opposition to the national income tax, for example, and would be expressed again by opponents of *Roe v. Wade* and other Supreme Court decisions and federal actions perceived to be acts of "social engineering."[10] The Civil War and the equal rights amendments to the Constitution following the war initiated the development of a genuinely national citizenship, opening the door to federal government action on a wide range of social and economic issues. Yet there was no adequate way for citizens to be represented directly in national government. Congressional representatives and senators were all tied to state and local territories and interests. Federal legislation in the interest of the country as a whole was, and remains, very difficult to come by.

The second qualification is that, regardless of people's attitudes toward federal action, a large percentage of Americans have understood their freedom as Americans to be something exercised by individuals able to decide how to organize their lives (without government's interference) in local communities, ethnic enclaves, small towns, and culturally distinct or class-based churches, clubs, and other organizations. The civil rights successes, whether welcomed or merely acceded to by whites, were not expected to change this picture radically. In other words, the majority might be willing to recognize as legitimate the legal right of African American *individuals*—like that of individual Italian Americans or Scandinavian Americans or Chinese Americans—to vote, own property, seek employment, form their own clubs, and organize religious institutions. However, in the view of most Americans this did not imply or require a radical reordering of society by judicial or legislative fiat from Washington. In fact, most northern whites felt that the American social, economic, and political order was legitimate in a way that they did not think southern slave society was legitimate. Once African Americans had the right to participate in society without legally enforced segregation, the majority of Americans expected that blacks would want the kind of society the majority already knew and accepted. This was the bias of both conservatives and most liberals and was tied up with a strong confidence in God's providential guidance of America from the founding through the Civil War and on into the American Century of democracy, freedom, and prosperity.[11]

The point here is simply that many Americans who were supportive of equal opportunity or civil rights for all did not envision federally compelled, social and economic "special treatment" for African Americans of a kind not given to white immigrants when they or their ancestors came to America and suffered deprivations. Whites, in this regard, failed to grasp the weight of the difference between African American history and the history of other immigrant groups. They underestimated the debt that they owed to African Americans who had not immigrated freely to this country. This was a debt that had mounted up over hundreds of years of slavery and forced segregation.

In contrast to this broad generalization about "most Americans," another sketch must be drawn to represent the outlook and expectations of most civil rights leaders and African Americans. Overcoming the illegitimate legal discrimination that African Americans had endured since the Civil War carried for this minority the hope of full inclusion in American society, a society they thought of, perhaps too naively, as a relatively homogeneous, socioeconomic enclave from which only blacks were excluded. Many blacks underestimated the extent to which "white" society was ethnically diversified, unintegrated, often-insecure, and class-divided. America, after all, had been the home of African Americans for hundreds of years, going back almost to the beginning of the colonial settlements. Slave ancestors had served inside the plantation houses and in the fields of white, land-owning families. They did not have their own social and economic world except on the fringes and underground. They had not been free immigrants to America, landing and working their way up independently. They were insiders, albeit as slaves, to white society in the South and they and their children had every reason to hope that once slavery ended, they would be *equal* insiders in the American household. They anticipated becoming full participants in precisely the kind of social and economic life that they had known from the inside but that had been denied them. This is what the civil rights reforms were supposed to achieve. Once the laws changed, all doors would be open. The hope of integration was a hope for full entry, for full "brotherhood" in one family under God in which whites and blacks together would share in the fulfillment of the American dream and the promise of a just and fully integrated kingdom of God in America. Black and white civil rights leaders encouraged these expectations by their visionary rhetoric of a new human community.[12]

This second generalization may be no more accurate in detail than the first as an oversimplified picture of a complex reality. Certainly there were significant differences among civil rights leaders and African Americans, just as there were among Americans generally. Those who broke away to form the Black Power movement, for example, had a different idea of pluralism and inclusion than those who adhered to King's ideals. Nevertheless, if these two generalizations have any warrant, they may help explain why the civil rights movement, led largely by black Christians with support from some white church leaders and people of other faiths, came so late in American history and then failed to hold together as a religiously energized civil rights movement after the initial successes of the 1950s and 1960s.

Andrew Michael Manis explains that in the decade from 1947 through 1957, the radical opposition between black and white Baptists over desegregation was rooted in a deeper American civil religion. For many white Protestants, America was, as G. K. Chesterton called it, "a nation with the soul of a church." By contrast, Manis quotes James Melvin Washington as saying that many black Baptists saw themselves as "a church with the soul of a nation."[13] The common ground of these two viewpoints is America—a promised land, modeled to some degree after biblical Israel's promised land. By the 1950s, the land was beginning to look like a threatened territory to many white Christians who identified America as the land given by God to the original covenant people (not including blacks and native Americans). To many blacks, on the other hand, the same land was becoming more and more the place where God's promise of freedom would soon be fulfilled and the truths of the Declaration of Independence realized for all Americans. White Baptists looked back; black Baptists looked forward.

In their conflict over desegregation, however, both blacks and whites depended on a civil religion that was not "differentiated from either the religious or the political systems of the society."[14] Their deepest political ideologies did not adequately come to grips with the actual differentiated condition of society. America represented God's grant of freedom to individuals, as many whites saw it. America was God's one people—one family—without color lines, as many blacks saw it. On the one hand, a majority of Americans, including white Christians, could eventually accept the achievement of civil rights for blacks (meaning that individual blacks would no longer be singled out by the law for discriminatory treatment), but they did not expect racial harmony to be produced by means of federal interference in every sphere of society in order to bring about one big family. They believed in a political order that protected individual freedom, private property, and social diversity, not in an American community that homogenizes all diversity and trumps all their social, cultural, and economic freedoms. They came to believe, or at least to accept, that African Americans should be allowed to enjoy the same constitutional rights they enjoyed, but that did not mean government and the courts should have authority to engineer change everywhere in society.

On the other hand, those—including Christians—who had the grandest expectations about civil rights reform, which was supposed to lead to the full integration of the American community, would not be satisfied until racial inequality was completely eliminated everywhere. And the chief institutions to which they continued to look to bring about change were the federal government and the courts over against the recalcitrant states.

Judging Between Expectations

There are truths on both sides of the contrast drawn above, truths that were not, and have not yet been, brought together into a single reform movement. To bring them together is, it seems to me, one of the important tasks, of a Christian-democratic civic movement of citizens of all races. The truth on one side is that a constitutionally limited government and legal system should protect and support a society of differentiated institutions, ethnic communities, churches, and diverse civic movements, the latter being free to contend with one another in public debate and election campaigns over the task and limits of government itself. The health and well-being of most nongovernmental organizations and relationships should be worked out within each one, on their own terms, in relative independence, and cannot be forced by government. The United States is, and should be, a pluralistic polity. To say this is not to advocate a laissez-faire attitude on the part of government. Rather, it is to argue as a matter of principle that a just government is one that upholds the rights, and respects the independent responsibilities, of individuals and nongovernment institutions and relationships. The United States as a political *unum* is not an undifferentiated community—one large family—in which government and the courts serve as all-pervasive, omnicompetent authorities.

The truth on the other side is that racism violates the integrity of creatures made in the image of God and is wrong everywhere, in every institution and relationship. The challenge in seeking to overcome racism, then, is to advance this second truth while avoiding the error of disregarding the first truth, a disregard that is evident when citizens try to use legal and political means to bring about an end to racism everywhere without discriminating carefully among the different kinds of responsibilities humans have.

Those who cling to the first truth about limited government and the relative freedom of independent institutions and free associations may resist and close their hearts to the force of the second truth. They may be slow to challenge racism with appropriate nongovernmental means and slow to accept rightful government action simply because it is taken by government. However, those compelled by the second truth to seek the end of racism everywhere in society by political and legal means may be slow to see the violation of the independent responsibilities of nongovernmental institutions and associations when government acts inappropriately. Each side produces a reaction from the other, pushing one another toward error rather than toward the element of truth that each harbors. Those resisting too much government intrusion and social engineering end up resisting even legitimate efforts by government to redress the injustices of legalized racism. Those seeking to overcome racism everywhere become convinced that any resistance to their efforts is evidence of racism.

If, in looking back on the last fifty years, contemporary anti-discrimination leaders, including Christians, focus on the second truth and judge that all resistance to legal/political reform efforts is due to deep-seated racism, they will more than likely keep fighting by political and legal means to eliminate every inequality they see between blacks and other Americans. If, however, those, including Christians, who believe that racism is wrong can also recognize that some of the resistance to certain civil rights reform efforts has been due not to deep-seated racism but to the feeling or conviction that some of those reform efforts have actually caused other injustices, then the reformers may conclude that a different assessment of the situation and a different approach to ongoing reform may be necessary. In this case, the aim should not be to go soft on racism but to recognize that racism must be opposed by many different means appropriate to, and built on respect for, the diversity of institutions and responsibilities that all people have in our society.

In what follows I hope to try to show how the two truths hang together from a Christian-democratic pluralist point of view, arguing that anti-discrimination efforts should be incorporated into the larger quest for public justice in a complex, differentiated society.[15] One of the great tests of twenty-first-century America will be whether Christians of all colors and races can overcome their biases and the inertia of past habits and ideologies to cooperate in new ways in all of the institutions and relationships that express the image of God.

Anti-discrimination and Education

Is it possible that the legal fight against racism in America could unintentionally cause injustice? Consider, by way of illustration, one of the most important arenas of social life—education—where the struggle for racial justice continues to this day, fifty years after *Brown v. Board of Education*.[16]

Since the 1960s, one of the means chosen to seek racial integration in society has been school integration, with heavy dependence on busing. As long as attention is focused only or chiefly on the legal requirement of equal treatment of all child-aged citizens within a publicly owned enterprise, then the attempt to integrate public schools by means of busing appears to be an entirely rational reform effort. If every citizen should be treated equally before the law, if all children are citizens and must attend school, and if schools are part of the civic commons controlled by government, then what could be more rational than to try to overcome racial separateness and unequal treatment by proportionately mixing differently colored children throughout publicly controlled schools? If the variables to be considered are simply school-aged citizens of all colors, on the one hand, and all available public school buildings, on the other, then a rational answer is for the public authorities to find technical means (buses) to disperse the children in a manner that achieves integration.

However, what if additional variables must be considered in order for government to do justice to the education of children of all races and colors? What if justice must also, at the same time, be done to families, neighborhoods, social networks, and religious communities that are not directly owned or controlled by public authorities? What if busing, despite its intent to remedy racial injustice, creates or aggravates other injustices, which are also injustices to African Americans? The fact is that many integrationist busing attempts have failed to achieve the aim of overcoming racial discrimination and have provoked angry reactions from parents, including African American parents. Why? Because schooling does, in fact, have to do with several different institutions and responsibilities. It involves parental child-rearing responsibilities and family well-being, including close connections among families, among parents and teachers, and between some families and their neighborhoods. Busing has often done damage to these relationships, separating families from the schools their children attend, dividing neighborhoods, and weakening the connection between teachers and the families and the connection between parents and children.[17]

One might argue that all the negative reactions to busing have arisen solely or chiefly because of racism on the part of whites. However, what if the negative reactions to busing have arisen not because of racism and not because most whites object to blacks receiving an equal education, but because, for example, parents, regardless of race and ethnic background, do not want their children bused far from home or to a school serving a community that is culturally foreign to them?[18] And what if there are other ways to achieve a more equal educational opportunity for all children of all races, ways that can also do justice to the diversity of the social, economic, religious, and other human variables? By raising this last question in a series of "what ifs," I am intentionally opening the door to a different approach to civil rights reform.

Promoting the Cause of Racial Justice

What contribution can a Christian-democratic approach make to the achievement of racial justice in American society today? Cooperation in the civil rights movement of the 1960s among black and white Christians and people of other persuasions contributed little to the development of a public philosophy sufficient to deal with life in a differentiated society in a unified republic—a public-legal *unum* responsible to uphold religious diversity and institutional differentiation. The movement and its impact reaffirmed the normative standards of the Bill of Rights for individual citizens, overcoming the blatant injustices that excluded African American individuals from equal treatment under the law. Beyond that, however, the movement left largely intact the idea that politics is either a means to the ends pursued by free individuals or a means to the end of creating a more socially integrated American family. The movement left largely intact the competing civil-religious visions held by many white and black Americans, that is, the vision of a nation with the soul of a church, on one side, and the vision of a church with the soul of a nation, on the other. Consequently, the particular identity, quality, and limits of the political order as a differentiated public community of citizens distinct from and yet related to nongovernment spheres of life, was not sufficiently grasped or promoted, and thus the cause that unified those who locked arms in the civil rights struggle lost much of its steam after the civil rights movement won some landmark victories. When the goal of a fully integrated and equal American community did not materialize, the movement that had successfully brought together opponents of legalized racism was not strong enough to maintain a wider, ongoing political movement for the reconstruction and ongoing construction of a just society.

In contrast to the various denominations of American civil religion, with their competing but largely undifferentiated national moralities and political pragmatics, I believe Christian faith calls citizens to the kind of prophetic political responsibility that is incompatible with any version of civil-religious nationalism or racism and opposed to any mode of politics that does not answer to the demands of justice for a differentiated society.[19] On the one hand, this means that both white and black Christians must relinquish utopian dreams of an undifferentiated national community, particularly of America as God's new Israel or as the coming Kingdom of God on earth. They must also relinquish liberal ideology, which holds that the United States is simply a rights-protecting entity that makes room for individual freedom in the market and not much more. Our republic can be just and do justice only as a community of citizens under public law. A just polity is one that upholds equal and fair treatment under law for people of all races as they exercise responsibilities in their families, churches, schools, businesses, and other organizations. A just polity is one that recognizes and gives equal treatment to people of all faiths, all colors, and all ethnic backgrounds, but it cannot overcome all sin or bring in the Kingdom of God to America.

The Christian-democratic basis for this approach is the biblical teaching that God upholds creation for all creatures and sends rain and sunshine on the just and unjust alike. Christians are supposed to live in tune with this will of God and work for equal treatment of all civic neighbors in the public order as well as to love their neighbors in every other kind of personal and organizational relationship. Christ's followers have no authority to try to separate wheat and tares in the field of this world (Matt. 5:43–48; 13:24–30, 36–43; Rom. 12:11–21). This is the biblical basis of Christian-democracy over against "Christian" imperialism, "Christian" statism, and "Christian" racist nationalism.

Taking into consideration the diversity of faiths, the diversity of races, and the diversity of institutions and organizations in our complex society, how can justice be done to all of them at the same time? In what respect can a pluralist perspective offer more hope for equal justice than can other viewpoints?[20] Without due attention by government to people as whole persons, created in the image of God, and not defined first of all by their color—without this kind of attention justice cannot be done to citizens who are always more than citizens. Race cannot be abstracted from the complex and diversified institutional character of our society in which different races share the same political community.

What would be the implications for racial justice if each state in the American union combined the two principles of confessional and structural pluralism, just summarized, in dealing with education? As I will explain in more detail in the next chapter, government can do justice to the educational needs of all citizens only by recognizing that families and schools are differentiated institutions with their own qualifications and responsibilities, distinct from the political order of citizens under law. Government cannot do justice to citizens of any race or color by treating either family or school as a branch or instrumentality of the state. In addition to recognizing the institutional diversity of society, government must also do justice to the diverse range of religious/philosophical views and cultural aims of its citizens. Whether or not citizens are traditionally and explicitly religious, their faiths, philosophies, and cultural aims should not be used as the basis for discriminatory public treatment against them as citizens. Public justice must be done to all families with their diverse views of life, and any inequity (for example, in educational funding, when government collects taxes for such a purpose) will be unjust to those families who are excluded from, or compelled against their will to conform to, the majority's uniform schooling option. This should hold for all families of whatever race or culture.

One reason why some parents, whether black or white, might choose one school over another is for religious or cultural reasons. A poor African American family that wants to educate its children in a thoroughly Muslim or a thoroughly Christian way should not be discriminated against because the family is black, or because it is poor, or because it is Muslim or Christian. And each of these qualifications requires a different level of consideration. Government does not do justice to this family if it excludes it from public benefit or legal protection because it is black. That is the primary principle established by *Brown v. Board of Education*. Neither is justice served if the family is ignored or left without educational choice because it is too poor to purchase the education it wants. Justice also fails if the family suffers educational discrimination because of its Muslim or Christian view of life. An attempt to secure racial equality in a way that violates the family's values, or educational choices, or religious freedom is not just.

Conclusion

A Christian public philosophy is needed to articulate the meaning of a public-legal *unum* of the state or political community—our republic—which upholds the full diversity of people in our differentiated society. Many of the economic, educational, familial, and health-care needs of racial minorities cannot, and should not, be addressed by legal and political means that preselect race as the qualifier and then use economic, educational, or other means to try to overcome the inequalities. The reason is that in a justly differentiated society, educational, ecclesiastical, familial, and economic institutions do not exist as the means to racist or anti-racist ends. Those institutions and organizations have their own ends and qualifying purposes, and justice must be done to them on their own terms. At the same time, there is every reason for government to address the causes of public-policy injustices in economic, educational, and health-care arenas, and to make sure that no legal barrier stands in the way of equal rights for African Americans and every other racial or cultural minority in the country.

Once citizens of color are not singled out for publicly enforced exclusion or negative discrimination because of their color, the manner and means of their inclusion must come about in ways that do justice to the responsibilities and standards appropriate to institutions and relationships that are not racially or politically qualified. A Christian-democratic approach that brings together blacks and whites (and people of other colors and cultures) will entail working actively in politically organized ways and in cooperation with other citizens to reform government and all of its public policies to achieve justice for all.

CHAPTER SIX

~~~

Equal Education for All

American schooling faces so many difficulties that some wonder whether the United States will be able to retain its edge in the increasingly competitive global economy. Even if the United States thrives, many worry about the growing distance between our well-educated and our poorly educated citizens—between those who will make it in an information economy and those who may not. On top, or perhaps at the bottom of all this, is evidence of a growing diversity in our society. Perhaps we have entered a stage of history where the diversity of cultures, viewpoints, and talents is so great that a single "common school" no longer makes sense.[1]

After several decades of attempts to reform education by political and legal mandates, a growing number of critics are now arguing that all such efforts to stem "the rising tide of mediocrity" will fail because they do not go to the root of the system's difficulties.[2] The fault with the entire system, according to John Chubb and Terry Moe, for example, is to be found precisely in its centralized political and bureaucratic structure.[3] According to these and other critics, an open system of plural choice that uses market mechanisms and puts control in the hands of individual schools and parents will have to be instituted before good schools can become the rule rather than the exception across the country.[4]

However, every argument for fundamental system reform immediately runs up against the criticism that an open system of school choice will aggravate at least two severe injustices. First, it will aggravate racism and/or the exclusion of the most needy students in our society.[5] Second, it will violate the First Amendment's establishment clause because public monies will end up in the hands of religious schools.[6] The key concern of public education, say those who defend the current system, should be common schooling that brings diverse children together, as Americans, for the future harmony of American society. Market competition and publicly supported school choice will only aggravate the fracturing of our society by encouraging racism, religious conflict, and acceptance of the growing gap the between rich and poor.

Clearly, the contemporary dilemmas and difficulties of American schooling and the designs for its reform involve basic issues of religious freedom, racial justice, equity and fairness for parents and educators, economic opportunity, and the future of wealth and poverty in American society.

A Glance at History

Writing in the 1970 U.S. Supreme Court case of *Lemon v. Kurtzman* (403 U.S. 602), Justice William O. Douglas commented:

> While the evolution of the public school system in this country marked an escape from denominational control and was therefore admirable as seen through the eyes of those who think like Madison and Jefferson, it has disadvantages. The main one is that a state system may attempt to mold all students alike according to views of the dominant group and to discourage the emergence of individual idiosyncrasies (630).

Four years later, in *Meek v. Pittenger* (421 U.S. 349), Justice William Rehnquist objected to the court majority's reasoning as follows:

> The Court apparently believes that the Establishment Clause of the First Amendment not only mandates religious neutrality on the part of government but also requires that this Court go further and throw its weight on the side of those who believe that our society as a whole should be a purely secular one. Nothing in the First Amendment or in the cases interpreting it requires such an extreme approach to this difficult question (395).

These two comments expose some of the key issues at stake in a struggle over the governance of schooling that dates back to the early nineteenth century, when a new public philosophy emerged to support an experiment in publicly organized and funded education. That philosophy, which I described in chapter 4 as essential to the second order and third order of American pluralism, was shared, in its essential features, by Thomas Jefferson, Noah Webster, Benjamin Rush, and Horace Mann, among others.[7] It has continued to influence the language and reasoning of Supreme Court decisions and public debate to the present day and is only now beginning to face serious challenge.[8]

Jefferson and other early American leaders were concerned about the future vitality of the republic. If the young country were to experience a growing diversification of states, families, churches, and schools, these leaders wondered whether the nation could hold together without some means of inculcating and promoting common republican virtues. The answer to which many of them came was the common public school.[9] An important aspect of their answer depended on their assumption that government could and should legitimately develop schools as an extension of its responsibility to promote common citizenship and republican values. That assumption goes back to Greek and Roman traditions that were revived during the Renaissance and imbibed by many of the educated leaders of eighteenth-century Europe and America. Jefferson and others came to believe that in the years to come the new republic could not depend on the existing and quite often informal efforts of moral and civic education in families and churches. A common school was needed to bind citizens in each state together in support of republican values. The idea that education should be an integral function of the political order did not arise in a vacuum but was part of a more embracing philosophy of society and of the political community itself.

For our purposes here, we will focus primarily on Jefferson's approach to public education in the early republic in order to elaborate the public philosophy that would have so much influence in the years to come. In Jefferson's thinking there are two centers of gravity in human affairs: the first is the individual person; the second is the universal law of nature embracing both physical necessity and moral obligation.[10] These two centers of gravity function dialectically, for they are dependent on one another while at the same time existing in tension with one another, like two poles of a planet's magnetic field.[11] The *individual*, in Jefferson's view, possesses rights and autonomy by virtue of, and in relation to, a *universal* moral sense. We might say that the moral law, which individuals experience through their moral sense, is the law of their freedom, the law that each should be free to actualize.[12]

A seldom-noticed characteristic of Jefferson's philosophy is that it lacks a clear and definite idea of what a republic, or state, or political community should be and what it should be qualified to do. And he has even less to say about the differentiated identities and distinct purposes of family, school, church, and economic enterprise. The omission is due largely to Jefferson's indebtedness to the Stoics who thought of individuals, natural law, and a universal moral sense without high-definition distinctions among the diverse institutions and organizations of society.[13] A society, in other words, has as its two main reference points the individual and the organized public community, both of which should comport with the natural law. The highest, or largest, or most universal institution compatible with individual rights and freedoms is a republic, but it has no definable limits save to guarantee the rights and property of its citizens and to guard the commonwealth of which they are a part. Jefferson and other advocates of the republic took for granted that individual citizens would not confront problems of conflicting allegiances to their homes, schools, churches, and businesses as long as their actions accorded with rational, moral principles.

The individual, from this point of view, has a natural right to live free of all bondage and subjection except to the moral law. At some points in Jefferson's writings, he emphasizes the priority of the individual as moral actor.[14] At other points, he stresses the republic as the highest embodiment of moral humanity.[15] As an individual, each person is bound only by the moral sense—conscience. On the other hand, within the public realm, a single will of the majority directs the society as if it were a one-willed moral being, bound by the same moral principles. The rights of individuals to conduct their lives freely should be protected at one pole, just as the right of the majority to carry the republic forward in freedom should be recognized at the other pole. In the public arena the minority willingly submits to the will of the majority, as if to its own highest rational and moral will.

The rationale for a common school springs from this philosophy. Jefferson, Mann, and others assumed, on the one hand, that the rational and moral autonomy of each individual must be respected and nurtured: thus the need for schooling. At the same time, they believed the republic could only hang together with a common will: thus the need for common schooling that would teach all citizens republican values. Education, then, should be the process whereby individuals are brought to maturity—each to his or her own independence as well as to a common sharing in the universal, rational, and moral order of the republic. Education should be treated as an extension of the republic, whose aim is to bring its immature citizens both to individual and to republican maturity. Jefferson and others who advocated the establishment of common schools did not believe that these schools would be the cause of any unjust discrimination against families, independent schools, and churches. To the contrary, they assumed instead that the moral training conducted in most homes, churches, and independent schools was private training and thus insufficient for the maturation and endurance of the republic. Parental responsibility in education should remain subservient to the more universal association of individuals in the republic for the common good of all.[16]

Writing to John Adams in 1813, Jefferson explained that his plan for education in Virginia was part of a larger program to replace an "artificial aristocracy" (including the clergy) with a "natural" one.[17] In much the same way that Jefferson thought kings and wealthy aristocrats tyrannized people's lives and properties, he believed the clergy tyrannized people's minds.[18] He wanted Virginia and the United States to rise above all tyrannies and elevate the people to freedom and self-rule. This program could succeed only if an equality of condition could be nurtured among the people, raising all of them to that level where they would be able by their own powers and judgment to select their own best peers for the direction of their government. This could be achieved, he believed, by means of a publicly supported common education for every citizen, except, of course, for the slaves who were not considered to be fully or equally human or deserving of a rational-moral education.

Notice the tension here between individual freedom and the common molding of all citizens. This is the tension highlighted in Justice Douglas's remark in the *Lemon v. Kurtzman* decision, quoted above. For Jefferson, the free individual would be the "perfectly homogeneous" American.[19] Each person would become mature and free by sitting at the feet of the government-appointed, natural educational aristocrat who would help raise all to an equality of condition.

Note also that the polar framework of this philosophy is not necessarily connected to the polarity of religion and secularity. The connection between the individual/universal polarity and the sacred/secular polarity was not firmly established until after the 1840s. In fact, for Jefferson, the common schools would definitely be inculcating religious and moral values.[20] They would not be neutral or secular in our contemporary sense of those terms. The important distinction for Jefferson was between, on the one hand, the universal, natural moral order, represented in society by the republic and its majority will, and, on the other hand, the realm of individual freedom in which people should be free to act without direction by government, aristocrats, or the church, so long as they heeded the moral sense within them. What Jefferson wanted to elevate in public and what he wanted to keep in private can be distinguished, respectively, as the universal or nonparochial, on the one hand, and the parochial, on the other. The natural law connected with the common moral sense was also clearly connected to nature's God, and thus the religious and moral character of a common school education would be universal and not parochial.

Of course, these distinctions make sense only from the point of view of Jefferson's philosophy. And that is precisely what allows us to see, at a later point in history, how fully dogmatic and parochial that philosophy really is.

Although Jefferson believed that his republican philosophy was common and universal, it was, in fact, but one among many possible viewpoints. Jefferson's plan, if successful, would amount to nothing less than the public establishment of an educational system that would allow a dominant faith or moral viewpoint to exclude all others in the public realm. In some of his private letters, Jefferson showed an awareness of his bias. For example, he "confessed his hope that the changes brought about by a public school system would include 'a quiet euthanasia of the heresies of bigotry and fanaticism which have so long triumphed over human reason.'"[21] Though Jefferson would not have called his convictions dogmatic, believing them to be simply the truth, his plan would substitute the dogma of rationalistic empiricism and enlightened moralism for the "Christian" dogmas that were, at the time, guiding many families, schools, and churches.[22]

My aim here is not to debate the extent of Jefferson's parochialism but rather to show how his philosophy guided him and others to their political and educational conclusions. Those conclusions, in turn, laid the foundations for the common, government-established school system in the various states. Jefferson's philosophy and the subsequent establishment of the common school, I contend, lie at the root of conflicts over religion, morality, and the control of schooling that have continued up to the present day.

Nineteenth- and Twentieth-Century School Controversies

During the 1840s, the jousting between religious groups and thinkers such as Horace Mann began to delineate the battle lines of the great school wars that were fought in New York and Boston.[23] That is when the connection was made between the private/public distinction and the sectarian/nonsectarian distinction. New York and Boston were experiencing large Catholic immigrations. Many white Anglo-Saxon Protestants (WASPs) feared that the common public order was threatened. When Catholics began to appeal for public support of their schools on the same basis that the Protestant schools received support for theirs, the fears of the majority mounted. The WASP majority in each city reacted to the pluralizing threat by making the argument that their own schools were common and "nonsectarian" but that the Catholic schools were parochial and "sectarian." By local and state political means, they engineered the circumstances to give public backing and funding only to the so-called nonsectarian common schools.[24]

At the time, no one thought of these common schools of the majority as secular or nonreligious. The majority's successful effort against the Catholics, however, led to the institutionalization of a system of government-established, government-funded, government-run schools acceptable to the majority and distinguished from what they called the sectarian schools of the Catholic immigrants. The public-legal consequence was to establish the distinction between public common schools and private sectarian schools. Both sets of schools served the public purpose of training citizens, and both were religiously biased—one largely Protestant, the other largely Catholic. One system, however, was established by public law as part of the nonsectarian, nonparochial, common public order within the framework of Jefferson's philosophy, while the other was relegated to the arena of private, sectarian choice and subjected to legal and financial discrimination. As American society diversified and became more secularized over the next hundred years, the common public schools changed to reflect the changing public opinion of the political majority. Given the framework established in the 1840s, there seemed to be no alternative to the gradual elimination of various aspects of the common schools that did not accord with majority will, on the one hand, and with the legal protection of individual rights, on the other.

The Supreme Court heard very few school cases before the 1940s, but the 1925 case of *Pierce v. Society of Sisters* (268 U.S. 510) is central to both this area of law and to the argument of this chapter. In *Pierce*, the Court upheld the right of parents to choose schools for their children other than those established by the State of Oregon, a right that had been denied by an Oregon law.[25] On the face of it, the Court's decision would seem to contradict what I have just argued, namely, that a public school monopoly, founded on the Jeffersonian philosophy, had come to dominate American schooling after the 1840s. According to *Pierce*, parents *do* have a fundamental right to choose the agency of education for their children. The educational "principalship" of parents for their children must be respected, said the Court.[26] This decision seems to call into question the state's preeminent right to appoint the agencies for the education of its citizens.[27] The parental right of choice must be allowed to stand, the Court ruled.

In fact, however, the *Pierce* case simply brought to light the contradictions and inequities inherent in what by that time was already a well-established system. The Court in *Pierce* did not overturn state primacy in education. It merely assured parents of their right to *opt out* of the public system if they could afford to do so and if conscience required it. Full parental *principalship* in public education was not acknowledged. Oregon was allowed to continue the practice of channeling all public funds and public recognition to its own agencies of education. After *Pierce*, Oregon merely had to tolerate the private right of parents to opt out of the public system at their own additional expense.

The situation in our day is essentially this: state and local governments (with federal and judicial support) assume the *principal* responsibility for the schooling of all citizens. Those governments generally seek to fulfill their educational responsibility by means of their own state-established *agencies*—the public common schools, for which they collect taxes from all property owners. Within this legal framework for education, the authority of parents over their children is incorporated into the general *civic* governing structure of the local public school. In other words, with respect to the education of children, the state assumes that parents will exercise their responsibility by way of their membership in the political community where they can vote for school board members as well as for local, state, and federal officials. Parental principalship in education, consequently, is almost entirely swallowed up in government's principalship. By definition, public agencies (the common schools) are treated as *belonging* to parents by virtue of their citizenship. Parents' responsibility for their children in education is to be fulfilled through civic institutions—the common school. If parents do not choose this preferred, responsible route, then parent's education of their children becomes a matter of private freedom not public obligation and must be at private expense.

The Contemporary Predicament

The distinctions that now exist in the laws governing education in the United States represent multiple ambiguities, contradictions, and historical accidents that continue to produce confusion and stir up controversy. The most recent Supreme Court decisions, such as the Cleveland voucher case in 2002, are only beginning to chip away at the confusion. The Court has been trying for years, for example, to decide how much government money can be channeled to the secular aspects of private religious education.[28] It has also repeatedly faced the opposite problem of how much "religious" activity can be carried on within the public secular schools.[29] The Court has not been able to resolve these and other unanswerable questions, such as how much freedom parents and teachers may enjoy inside the public schools, or what kind of public purpose is served by private schools, or how much religious opinion a public school teacher may convey as a matter of her First Amendment rights.

To illustrate the predicament that has not yet been resolved by the Supreme Court, consider its 1963 decision, *Abington School District v. Schempp* (374 U.S. 203). The Court struck down a Pennsylvania law that required Bible reading in the public school. According to the Court, the Pennsylvania law violated the establishment clause of the First Amendment. Writing the majority opinion, Justice Clark said:

The place of religion in our society is an exalted one, achieved through a long tradition of reliance on the home, the church, and the inviolable citadel of the individual heart and mind. We have come to recognize through bitter experience *that it is not within the power of government to invade that citadel, whether its purpose or effect be to aid or oppose, to advance or retard. In the relationship between man and religion, the state is firmly committed to a position of neutrality* (226, emphasis added).

Justice Clark here takes for granted that religion is unambiguously private and exists entirely outside the public order. That assumption led him to overlook one of the central institutions in our society that had, until recently, helped to exalt religion in American society, namely, the public common schools. He refers to the home, church, and individual heart as the great centers of religion. But this is simply a repetition of the central dogma of Jeffersonian philosophy, augmented as it was by the secular/sectarian distinction of the mid-nineteenth century. The truth is that schools, both government-run and independent, were the centers of Christian training for decades into the nineteenth century, and even by the end of the last century, Protestantism controlled the ethos of the so-called nonsectarian schools.

Justice Clark also had no doubt that government *can* be neutral toward the "citadel of the individual heart and mind" while it simultaneously controls and finances the government-run school system that shapes young hearts and minds. And yet, the government-established common schools, controlled by local and state institutions, are not and never have been religiously neutral. They were not designed to be neutral as Jefferson and others conceived them; they were not neutral when they were controlled by Protestants; they were not neutral when Bible reading *was* required; and they are not neutral today even though the dominant secularist ideology insists that they are.[30]

The question that Justice Clark apparently did not consider is one that goes to the underlying assumptions of the philosophy he simply took for granted. Can the state be neutral with regard to "the relationship between man and religion" while it prejudicially funds and governs one system of schools and discriminates against all others? Can the state claim to be acting with neutrality toward religion at the same time that it assumes to itself the prerogative of deciding what is and what is not religious?

My argument is that government *should* treat all of its citizens evenhandedly without discriminating against any of them for religious reasons. There is no question that justice demands this kind of equal treatment or nondiscrimination. But precisely in terms of evenhandedness and equal treatment, the present structure of education is unjust. The problem begins with the blinders that come with the ruling philosophy, which overlooks the independent social reality of families and schools. Governments and the Supreme Court have not yet adequately accounted for or begun to treat these institutions fairly and without discrimination. Governments have no right to predefine families and schools as being either sectarian or nonsectarian, either religious or secular, free only in private and not in public. The Constitution provides no basis for government to decide unilaterally to control schooling while ignoring the preexisting educational roles of families and nongovernment schools in that very arena. There is no just way to respect the educational process and the rights of families without treating the actual diversity of schools and families in a nondiscriminatory and equitable fashion. The effort to make education a single, exclusive, homogeneous service that governments deliver directly to citizens inevitably distorts the very nature of education. Children are not merely immature citizens in a republic. They are not mere creatures of the state. They are simultaneously children in homes, members of churches, students, playmates, and eventually employees and employers. The fundamental assumptions of Jefferson's philosophy are mistaken and inadequate to deal with a complex, institutionally differentiated, and religiously diverse society. John Chubb and Terry Moe are correct that the reform of schooling cannot succeed within the present system of governance.[31] But whereas Chubb and Moe emphasize market choice as the way to achieve a higher quality of schooling across the country, I wish to stress structural and confessional pluralism on the part of government as the way to achieve justice for all. If governments will do justice, they will also thereby open the way for parents to have real choice and for a variety of schools to have equal opportunity to serve the children of all families. This will indeed make it possible for schools to improve and to serve the needs and ambitions of families and children.

In the 1983 Supreme Court case *Mueller v. Allen* (463 U.S. 388), the Supreme Court upheld Minnesota's small effort to provide some tax relief to parents who send their children to nongovernment schools (402–403). However, the traditional legal rationale for both the state law and the Court's decision remained unchanged. Government continues to assume the role of principal in education and directs educational monies in a highly disproportionate measure to its own schools. Those who choose nonstate schools are still viewed as "opting out" of the public realm. Even though Minnesota parents who choose nongovernment schools now receive a degree of tax relief, the dollar amount remains minor compared with the benefits gained by public school parents. A little financial relief for private school parents only underscores rather than resolves the continuing inequity of the private/public, sacred/secular distinction.

Jefferson judged that a representative government that reflects the will of the majority may legitimately govern the republic—the public order—precisely because it represents the universal community of free, moral individuals.[32] Later on, this supposedly universal public community came to be called secular, over against the multiple religious groups that were allowed to flourish in private outside the common terrain of the republic. But why should this public order be called a secular thing? On what grounds does the government have a right to grant itself a monopoly over what it defines as secular? Does this mean that governmental sovereignty over everything secular should have no limits as long as individual rights in private are protected? Or, if we look at the matter from the opposite side, on what grounds does government have a right to decide that religion should belong primarily if not solely to churches or church-related institutions and to the privacy of the individual's heart and mind?

The First Amendment does not mention families and schools. In fact, it does not even mention churches. In the way the amendment is often interpreted, however, religion is identified with churches and private conscience, while government is presumed to have the right to exercise a monopoly over what it defines as secular. In school cases, the courts do not typically recognize families and schools as having independent identities and responsibilities separate from church and state or from the religious and the secular. Yet that is precisely the diversified structure of our complex society. Thus the predicament in which we find ourselves seems to allow for no escape. The institutionalization of schooling as a function or department of government, the formalizing of certain language categories, a much-disputed but still dominant public philosophy—all of these are among the elements intertwined in a complexity that has left the Supreme Court and the broader public in a state of confusion and ambiguity. What must be done?

The System Must Be Changed

Resolving these confusions and difficulties will require some important changes in the laws that govern education. That resolution is likely to emerge, however, only if certain fundamental assumptions change.[33] Let us begin with the assumption about principalship and agency in education.

Most of our common and statute laws take for granted that parents bear the principal responsibility for their minor children.[34] The major exception or exclusion to this rule occurs in the realm of education, as just noted. That exception is, I believe, an error and one of the basic causes of the present confusion in education policy. This is not to suggest that parents should hold omnicompetent control over their children and that government bears no responsibility for minors in their civic capacity. Parental principalship in the home does not mean isolated privatization of children. Children are also citizens who have basic rights that should be protected by government. But public justice for child-age citizens cannot be upheld by government if it denies or infringes the rights and responsibilities of parents for their own children who also happen to be citizens.

Parental principalship cannot be upheld without rejecting once and for all government's claim to that principalship in the sphere of education. The basic Jeffersonian assumption, revived in the Renaissance and dating back to ancient Greece, must be relinquished. This does not mean, however, the complete privatization of education. That would occur only if we continued to hold to the polar conception inherent in Jefferson's individualist/universalist philosophy. In place of that framework, I am contending for public recognition of the distinguishable rights of nongovernment institutions such as families and schools, along with the recognition of government's important responsibility for the public welfare of all citizens.

What are some of the implications of this shift in assumptions and outlook? First, public law would recognize people in society as more than just individuals and citizens. People would also be recognized as family members, church members, school members, and much more. With respect to the education of children, the proper response of government would then be to acknowledge the family, with its inherent parental responsibility for the care of minor children, and at the same time recognize its own responsibility for the public well-being of all citizens, families, churches, and so forth.

Second, going hand in hand with the shift that recognizes the family's identity and parental principalship in education there must also be a new acknowledgment of what constitutes an agency of education. Throughout American history, we have had many different kinds of schools. The government's own schools have never educated all children. Prior to the 1840s, most schools were independent of direct government management. Even after the 1840s, a significant percentage of American schools remained independent.[35] This fact alone demonstrates that educational agencies need not be government-owned and operated in order to function as agencies of an education that performs a public service. It also shows that a school is not, in the first place, an extension of government. In many if not all states of the union today, the law recognizes four different kinds of educational agency, all of which meet with approval as fulfilling a public educational purpose. They are government-run schools, parochial (church-run) schools, private (independent) schools, and home schooling. If we are really interested in understanding what constitutes "publicly legitimate schooling," we must recognize all four of these legally authorized agencies of education as contributors to the public education of America's children and future citizens.

The point here is that all of these agencies of education deserve just and equitable treatment by government. Under the existing polarized scheme of individual/universal, or private/governmental, however, schools are reduced either to privacy or to the extension of government's public monopoly when it comes to funding. This reduction makes it impossible to appreciate the unique identities of schools as distinguished from other nongovernmental and governmental institutions in society. It leads to ignorance of the public-purpose achievements of the nongovernment schools and often to a slighting of the educational (rather than the governmental) purpose of government-run schools. A school is an agency of education. It is built on a philosophy of education; it hires teachers trained in different disciplines; it stands *in loco parentis*[36] for minor children. A school, therefore, must master a particular, differentiated art that has to do with nurturing children toward intellectual (and other kinds of) maturity in a way that complements and wins the trust of parents who are responsible for those very same children. Students in a school take on a role that can be distinguished from that of a child in a family and a citizen in a state. Schools, in other words, are schools and not simply extensions of families or the government. They have a life of their own. To do justice to schools, therefore, government needs to acknowledge them in their own character just as it should recognize families as having their own identity and purpose. Government does not represent citizens as autonomous republican individuals. It deals with citizens who are at one and the same time also family members, school participants, and more.

The rightful recognition of schools as independent entities will not require that the government relinquish all responsibility for education. Once again, this would be the logical consequence only if we were to insist on the polar framework of individual/universal, private/governmental. To do justice to the agencies of education does not even require that government close down all of its own schools. Rather, government should begin to deal with schools, including its own, as distinct agencies of education rather than as an extension or department of government. Then it should do what a just government ought to do, namely, treat all agencies of education justly and without discrimination.

With respect to government itself, we also need a new perspective and some new assumptions. Government *does* have the responsibility to secure public justice for all its citizens in the political community. It bears responsibility for the public welfare and the well-being of the republic as defined by its civic community, legal system, police and defense functions, public health, and environmental health. However, all of this necessitates the protection of various human institutions and associations that are neither individual persons nor departments of state. Government's responsibility to uphold the rights of its citizens and the well-being of society means protecting individuals, families, churches, and schools from unjust discrimination. The Greek Orthodox Church should enjoy the same public rights and protections as the Presbyterians and the Baptists, Muslims, and Jews. A black child should have the same public rights and privileges as a white child.

When it comes to the education of citizens, therefore, government may well decide that fairness, equity, equal opportunity, and public well-being for all citizens necessitate a public requirement that every citizen should receive a free education, beginning at an early age. To promote this public purpose, government may, quite properly, decide to tax citizens widely and generally to raise the funds for a free education. Many questions about the education of citizens are proper for governments and legislatures to entertain and to answer, as long as the government's concern is with its responsibility for public justice. Having said this, however, my contention is that henceforth all of these questions and answers about government's actions ought to be dealt with in the framework of a new public-legal system for education that arises from the new pluralist assumptions outlined above. What would a new pluralistic system entail?

First, *parental choice* in the schooling of children would be upheld by government as a first principle, leading to the equitable treatment of all parents. The current form of choice allows parents either to use the district common school at no extra cost or to opt out of that system at their own expense. This choice, grounded as it is in the assumption of governmental principalship, is simply unfair and inequitable. For many with low incomes the choice does not exist, and it is an unfair choice even for those with sufficient incomes. If parents are truly the principals in the education of their children, then the only way government can do justice to them and to all child-age citizens is to accept and grant legal recognition to parental principalship for the purpose of choosing the means of education for children.

Second, this shift would require the just treatment of all agencies of education. The only way that parental choices of different educational agencies can be realized fairly and equitably is if the law no longer gives discriminatory favors to the government's own schools. In other words, coinciding with the recognition of parents as the principals in the education of their children, government would honor, without discrimination, those agencies of education that parents choose. Every school would have the same legal and financial opportunity to open its doors to the public.

There are numerous means by which a genuine diversity of schools can be treated equitably in public law. What should be clear from the argument above is that most current proposals for tax credits and vouchers, while intending to alleviate some of the financial burden of parents who want to use nongovernment schools, will not lead to full justice for parental principalship and diverse educational agencies. Vouchers might offer a first step in the direction of greater equity, but as long as government schools are treated as the only legitimate *public* schools, then public monies and legal privileges for private education will never be distributed in truly proportionate amounts. In fact, it is generally unjust for public funds to be spent for private purposes. Public funds should be spent for public purposes. Public support of education for all children is a public purpose and every child, wherever educated, deserves public support. The reason that educational tax credits or vouchers are even considered today is that most citizens recognize that nongovernment schools *do* serve a public purpose. But a token of public appreciation extended toward poor parents who would like to use those schools is not sufficient to meet the demands of justice. The way to deal with all schools justly, then, is to recognize the public service that all schools fulfill. This means treating all such agencies of education, both government-run and nongovernment schools, as eligible for parental selection without legal or financial discrimination.

Given the new set of assumptions and policy implications proposed above, what will happen if some parents select a school that happens to be run by a church or is grounded in an explicitly religious philosophy of education? If the government supports such a school, whether directly or indirectly, will it not become illegitimately entangled in religion or run the danger of establishing a religion?

To the contrary, the new framework articulated here shows that if government were *not* to allow parental choice of religious schools on the same basis as it allows choice of other schools, it would be discriminating against those parents and against some or all religions. An establishment danger would arise only if the government decided to give special benefit to those who attend the schools of one religious persuasion but not to those of another. In fact, an illegitimate religious establishment exists now by virtue of the fact that the government grants privileges to its own schools to the disadvantage of nongovernment schools. It thereby establishes a viewpoint or philosophy that displaces all others in public. Many now charge that the public schools in effect establish the philosophy or religion of secular humanism even as those schools once established White Anglo-Saxon Protestantism. Whatever the philosophy of education imposed in government-run schools, the effect is the same: a violation of the First Amendment's establishment clause. The only way to avoid an establishment of religion is to institute a fair and equitable distribution of education benefits (financial and otherwise) that follow parental choice among a diversity of schools.[37]

Government's general public purpose (the Supreme Court would say its "secular purpose") in promoting education is to enable every child to gain access to the schooling of his or her parent's choice. If the legislation that implements this purpose recognizes parental principalship and diverse educational agencies, then its "general public purpose" is fulfilled when parents are able freely to choose the school they want for their children without legal or financial penalty. If the conscience of some parents requires a Catholic parochial school, and the conscience of others leads them to a Jewish or Muslim school, and the conscience of others demands a nonreligious school, then government will have done justice to all parents and to all schools if it treats them all the same with proportionate funding and with the same legal recognition. No religion is thereby established.

By not discriminating among parental choices or schools, the government thereby achieves true neutrality or impartiality, which is neither indifference nor hostility toward the religion or nonreligion of any parent or school. And by recognizing schools as schools, and families as families, the government does not compromise the independence or integrity of any religious or nonreligious organization that happens to run a school, whether that organization is an educational association, a church, a state, or another kind of organization. Government keeps its attention focused on the promotion of the general, public purpose that all schools are supposed to serve.

In this respect, the entire issue of religion vs. secularity is dissolved and schooling is removed from the illegitimate bind in which it was placed beginning more than a century and a half ago. The contrast of religious/secular, sectarian/nonsectarian, was a mistaken dichotomy in the first place. It would never have become an issue had it not been for the way the nineteenth-century Protestants tried to exclude Catholic schools from public recognition on the grounds of their parochialism and sectarianism. It would never have become an issue if Americans had not mistakenly restricted the word "religion" for use only in referring to private, sectarian piety and church life. Religion cannot be thus confined. It is also the way many people choose to live, including the way they choose to raise and educate their children. Government has no constitutional right to predefine the limits and scope of religion. Nor does it have the concomitant right to grant itself a monopoly over the so-called secular world.

If, on all of these terms, government (1) no longer lays claim to principalship in the education of citizens, (2) recognizes with full equity the diverse range of educational agencies, and (3) treats schooling as schooling rather than as something divided between religious privacy and public secularity, then it can guarantee to every child the public protection and assistance demanded by the norm of public justice. Such protection and assistance fits quite naturally into the wider range of government's responsibilities to guarantee racial nondiscrimination, to protect educationally disadvantaged children, and to challenge state financing mechanisms that may be inequitable across localities, counties, and districts. Only by means of equitable pluralism in education can government uphold equal treatment of all citizens, all families, and all schools.[38] What is required in order to establish such a system of equitable pluralism for education, however, is a new public philosophy that can lead to what (in chapter 4) I called a fourth order of public pluralism. This is the burden of a Christian-democratic vision of state and society.

CHAPTER SEVEN

⌁

Liberalism and the Environment

"For a while," Robert D. Kaplan wrote in 1994, "the media will continue to ascribe riots and other violent upheavals abroad mainly to ethnic and religious conflict. But as these conflicts multiply, it will become apparent that something else is afoot, making more and more places like Nigeria, India, and Brazil ungovernable. . . . It is time to understand 'the environment' for what it is: *the* national-security issue of the early twenty-first century."[1] This will prove to be so, according to Kaplan, because of "surging populations, spreading disease, deforestation and soil erosion, water depletion, air pollution, and possibly, rising sea levels" (58).

Today, post-9/11, concern about terrorism in the United States all but drowns out serious consideration of environmental degradation as a threat to national and international security. Few would argue that the environment is *the* national-security issue of the early twenty-first century. Yet Kaplan's assertion cannot be dismissed too quickly. With growing populations in the Middle East and other parts of the world, the crises to which Kaplan points show no sign of abatement. In fact, the primary causes of ungovernability and even terrorism ten or twenty-five years from now could well be competition over water supplies and agricultural land rather than opposition to the American empire.

In the United States, we confidently assume that we will face no governability crisis. Environmental concerns will be dealt with as they arise by means of our always-flexible democratic, judicial, and free-market processes. Overpopulation in the Southwest that foments conflict over limited water supplies will be resolved by market forces, technological advances, and democratic bargaining. The receding Ogallala aquifer beneath midwestern farmland will not lead to disaster because new technologies and shifting populations will alleviate the pressures. Acid rain, shrinking wet lands, top-soil losses, and air pollution—these and every other environmental danger will be met by technologically advanced, market-oriented, pragmatic Americans who always find a way to solve problems.

Are there sufficient grounds, however, for this "can-do" optimism? With every passing year Congress appears to be more divided along ideological and partisan lines, it waits longer and longer to face critical policy choices, and it becomes ever more subject to the demands of interest-group brokering. Is this the kind of governance pattern that can produce sound, long-term decisions about environmental sustainability? If Washington has difficulty dealing with the long-term stability of Social Security and health-care insurance, what makes us think that environmental dangers will be handled adequately and in time? There are reasons to be skeptical and they have to do with the very foundations of liberalism—the dominant American political ideology—and the way liberalism's adherents pursue their causes in the American political system.

In American politics, the quest for environmental protection has arisen and positioned itself in the judicial and political bargaining processes as one interest among many. As a distinguishable matter of public concern, environmental protection depends on the strength of interest groups that make environmental protection their chief cause. For in the process of interest-group bargaining, environmental groups must compete with business, labor, agricultural, and energy interests, to name only the most prominent. *The Economist* magazine reported in 1991 (March 30), for example, that two of the biggest polluters in the United States are the defense and energy departments of the federal government. If environmental protection is to improve, the report continued, there would need to be a reduction or withdrawal of existing federal subsidies that encourage loggers in Alaska, irrigators in California, and cattle grazers in Nevada. In other words, environmentalists would have to gain an advantage over defense contractors, loggers, farmers, and ranchers in congressional battles, if environmental protection standards were to be adopted and maintained.

Is this the only way to pursue the quest for environmental protection? Should we simply take for granted this complex process of interest-group competition for government's attention and favors? Should citizens have to choose sides: either jobs or the environment, either cheaper food or the environment, either adequate energy supplies or the environment? If one has a business interest, does that mean one will inevitably have to leave environmental protection to others and probably find oneself opposing them? If one holds a high military position, does that free one from responsibility for the environment? And, on the other side, if one becomes a strong environmentalist, does that mean one will inevitably have to adopt an anti-business, anti-military, anti-energy-consumption mentality?[2] In answer to all these questions, it certainly appears that most Americans *do* take for granted precisely this approach to politics. But why is that so?

Absurdity or Standard Operating Procedure?

In order to track down the source of our American assumptions and habits, let's start with a concrete example and work back to its roots. Out of concern for the protection of Pennsylvania wetlands, state Senator David J. Brightbill proposed a law that he admitted would leave the "stickiest issue" for the courts (*Patriot News* [Harrisburg], 10 April 1991). That issue was how far government can go in taking the use of private property without delivering "adequate" compensation to the owner. Even in the best years, wrote the *Patriot News* editors, "the state does not have the money to compensate the owners of private wetlands who claim to be deprived of the right to put their swampland to its 'highest and best use.'" But isn't there something absurd, the editors asked, about the assumption that taxpayers should have to "compensate every property owner for the intrinsic merits of his land when left to the devices of nature," or that taxpayers should have to "compensate property owners for allowing trees to grow because they absorb carbon dioxide and produce oxygen to the benefit of the public and planet?"

Indeed, I would argue that there is something wrong here, *unless*, of course, one accepts the assumptions and patterns of behavior that belong to our current political system and predominant political ideology. If one starts with the classical liberal assumption that all rights and public governing authority arise from autonomous individuals and the contracts and property claims made by those free individuals, then one will not recognize any *prior* obligations to protect land, water, plants, or animals. If one starts with the assumption that efforts to protect the environment can arise only on the basis of prior property claims, then there is nothing absurd about the assumption that private property rights come first and public ecological well-being comes second. Environmental protection will necessarily be seen as growing from *human* conflict over competing human uses of natural resources and other creatures. Human obligations exist not in relation to an original, inherent need or value of the environment but only in relation to competing, self-chosen human designs on various properties. Thus, it is perfectly logical for a private property owner to assume that any outside "interference" in her property rights requires compensation (whether from government or from another individual) at the going market rate for the highest use to which she could profitably put her property.

The problem or the "absurdity" in this framework comes to light only if one steps outside of it, as the Harrisburg editors tried to do in asking why a property owner should be compensated for allowing trees to grow. For then it becomes evident that the ecological value of trees in the larger natural and social environment precedes the property owner's claims even if the discovery of that value appeared subsequent to the private ownership claim. A person's property right neither creates nor exhausts the value of what is owned. From this point of view, the limits of nature, which ought to have been part of the definition of property from the outset, should not have been disregarded when a legal right to certain property was granted. Instead, those limits should have been recognized as part of the definition of the stewardship obligations of one who would come to own the property.

Since the statements in the last paragraph are foreign to liberalism, however, we must try to understand liberal doctrine.[3]

What Has John Locke Done for Us?

While it is certainly true that John Locke (1632–1704) is not solely responsible for the structure of the American political system and the American version of liberalism, his philosophy has had a huge influence on our political practice. We must try to understand that influence.

For Locke, all humans were created by God in a state of equality, "without subordination or subjection" to one another (122).[4] Moreover, God gave "the world to men in common" along with reason, which is the law of nature. Humans are "to make use of [reason] to the best advantage of life and convenience. The earth and all that is therein is given to men for the support and comfort of their being" (134). In Locke's view, however, there is no divinely appointed responsibility of "men in common" to manage or govern the "earth and all that is therein." That which is universally common for individuals is the Maker's law of nature for individual freedom and rationality. "The state of nature," says Locke, "has a law of nature to govern it which obliges every one; and reason, which is that law, teaches all mankind who will but consult it that, being all equal and independent, no one ought to harm another in his life, health, liberty, or possessions" (123).

The meaning of the word "common" for Locke is that each person shares the same identity and liberty and is subject to the same law of nature, which is reason, and reason affirms the law of individual liberty. That which is universal, in other words, is the law of individual freedom, not a law that holds for a common responsibility that transcends or precedes individual liberty. "The natural liberty of man is to be free from any superior power on earth, and not to be under the will or legislative authority of man, but to have only the law of nature for his rule" (132). This is Locke's description of the naturally free person. Consequently, the only way that a common concern or common project can come up for rational consideration is through agreed-upon action among free individuals who have first acted in expression of their liberty to appropriate something in the world as individual possessions. That possession then becomes an extension of each person's possession of oneself. Locke explains it this way:

> Though the earth and all inferior creatures be common to all men, yet every man has a property in his own person; this nobody has any right to but himself. The labour of his body and the work of his hands, we may say, are properly his. Whatsover then he removes out of the state that nature hath provided and left it in, he hath mixed his labour with, and joined to it something that is his own, and thereby makes it his property. It being by him removed from the common state nature hath placed it in, it hath by this labour something annexed to it that excludes the common right of other men. For this labour being the unquestionable property of the labourer, no man but he can have a right to what that is once joined to, at least where there is enough and as good left in common for others (134).

Furthermore, "the taking of this or that part [out of the state of nature] does not depend on the express consent of all the commoners," but becomes "my property without the assignation or consent of anybody. The labour that was mine, removing them out of that common state they were in, hath fixed my property in them" (135).

It appears that Locke has begun with a genuine commons, given by God to humankind. However, the only human access to, or responsibility for, that commons is by means of the absolutely individual and private actions of those who, by nature, share nothing in common except the law of individual self-possession and the liberty that authorizes them to take reasonable, individual action. And when any individual "mixes his labor" with anything outside of himself, that which he takes hold of becomes an extension of his private property in his own person.

Now, there is a limit to what one may rightfully possess, according to Locke, namely "where there is enough and as good left in common for others." We'll return to this point later. Sticking with individual liberty and private possessions for the moment, we may ask whether there is anything for which individuals bear *joint* responsibility either in the development and use of their possessions or in the protection of themselves and their own properties. Locke answers that there is indeed a major institution that transcends individual freedom and private possession. It is civil government. Yet government is not something that existed prior to, or outside the bounds of, the original self-possession and self-government of individuals. Government is not something ordained by God above or as a condition for individual liberty. Individuals are not *naturally* political. Rather, government arises from a contractual agreement among self-possessing, autonomous individuals who create it.

Yet why would free individuals create and subject themselves to such an institution? Locke raises and answers this question in the following way:

> If man in the state of nature be so free, as has been said, if he be absolute lord of his own person and possessions, equal to the greatest, and subject to nobody, why will he part with his freedom, why will he give up his empire and subject himself to the dominion and control of any other power? To which it is obvious to answer that though in the state of nature he hath such a right, yet the enjoyment of it is very uncertain and constantly exposed to the invasion of others. . . . This makes him willing to quit a condition which, however free, is full of fears and continual dangers. The great and chief end, therefore, of men's uniting into commonwealths and putting themselves under government is the preservation of their property (184).

Quite clearly, the supposedly absolute freedom and self-possession of individuals is not so absolute after all. For free individuals cannot secure themselves. Yet Locke does not work backwards from his starting point to examine the limits, inadequacy, and dependency of human freedom or why God thus created man. He does not take into consideration all the human dependencies and interdependencies that make it possible for a person to come to maturity, nor does he consider any of the ecological conditions on which humans depend for life and the enjoyment of their possessions. Rather, his only serious consideration of limits to freedom is the limit posed by "the invasion of others," originating from every other person's freedom and self-possession. The equal freedom of others is what gives birth to fears and insecurity and dangers. Therefore, these free though fearful individuals decide to make an agreement, to negotiate a contract, that will establish an umpire who will protect each person's life and property from others (168–183). That umpire is what Locke calls civil government.

Contracting to create government does not come about because individuals do not already possess the right of self-defense and the right to punish those who would disturb their freedom and property. Each person has that right. Yet apart from a settled common law and an umpire to enforce that law on everyone equally, individuals will find themselves in a perpetual state of war. For that reason, rational individuals are willing, for the preservation of each one's freedom and possessions, to transfer their natural right of self-government to a common, civil government. That is what establishes political society. No political society can exist, says Locke, "without having in itself the power to preserve the property and, in order thereunto, punish the offences of all those of that society . . . where every one of the members hath quitted his natural power, resigned it up into the hands of the community in all cases that excludes him not from appealing for protection to the law established by it" (163).

Notice here for our purposes that the responsibility of government for political society arises only from the extension of individual property rights—the right that each individual has in his or her own person and possessions. There is no other commons or human community for which government has a transcendent or prior responsibility. In fact, the authority of the government is a mere extension of each person's self-government, much like property becomes a person's possession as an extension of each person's own self-possession. In one sense, then, we can say that for Locke there is no such thing as *public* authority or *public* government but only the consolidation of many private self-governments into a common or compound self-government. Locke puts it this way:

> [T]hough every man who has entered into civil society and is become a member of any commonwealth has thereby quitted his power to punish offences against the law of nature in prosecution of his own private judgment, yet, with the judgment of offences which he has given up to the legislative in all cases where he can appeal to the magistrate, he has given a right to the commonwealth to employ his force for the execution of the judgments of the commonwealth, whenever he shall be called to it; which, indeed, are his own judgments, they being made by himself or his representative (164).

The importance of this point both for interest-group politics and for environmental protection in the United States today cannot be overemphasized.

Each person gives up to the government the power to punish offenses against the law of nature, which is an offense against any person's freedom and private property, and yet that governmental power is, in an important sense, the extension of each person's original power to execute one's own judgments made through one's own representative, who is an extension of one's own liberty and property. Moreover, each person's dispossession of the power of individual self-government entails the ability to "appeal to the magistrate" on behalf of one's own interests and judgment in accord with the law of reason, which is the law of one's own freedom and self-government.

This act of creating political society, says Locke, is what takes individuals out of the state of nature and into a commonwealth. The government of the commonwealth is thus "a judge on earth, with authority to determine all the controversies and redress the injuries that may happen to any member of the commonwealth; which judge is the legislative, or magistrate appointed by it" (164). The government thus has genuine power and is supported by the obligation that each member of the society must now yield to the majority determination of what the law should be (169). Yet no rational person would enter into a political society that did not have as its purpose to support and protect each individual's life and property. The word "commonwealth" thus means little more than a combination of many "privatewealths." According to Locke:

> But though men when they enter into society give up the equality, liberty, and executive power they had in the state of nature into the hands of the society, to be so far disposed of by the legislative as the good of the society shall require, yet it being only with an intention in every one the better to preserve himself, his liberty and property—for no rational creature can be supposed to change his condition with an intention to be worse—the power of the society, or legislative constituted by them, can never be supposed to extend farther than the common good, but is obliged to secure every one's property by providing against [the] defects . . . that made the state of nature so unsafe and uneasy. And so whoever has the legislative or supreme power of any commonwealth is bound to govern by established standing laws, promulgated and known to the people, and not by extemporary decrees; by indifferent and upright judges who are to decide controversies by those laws; and to employ the force of the community at home only in the execution of such laws, or abroad to prevent or redress foreign injuries, and secure the community from inroads and invasion (186).

What is clear from this is that government's authority exists to protect the private property, lives, and freedom of those who contracted to create it. And any controversies over those laws are to be decided by upright judges who have no other aim or purpose. Only after individuals have mixed their labor with the things God created does any property come into existence. And government's task arises only after these property-possessing individuals decide to give government the job of protecting each one's life and possessions.

Entirely foreign to Locke's thinking—and to liberalism to this day—is recognition of a direct obligation of government, from the outset, to protect the commons (defined as more than multiple private properties) from misuse by property-possessing individuals and for the long-term good of all, including future generations. Government has no existence, no divinely ordained responsibility, prior to its creation by and for the individuals who created it in order to protect themselves and their property. Government is answerable to its creators—self-possessing individuals—and to the law of nature, which is reason, to protect individual life and property. There is nothing else.

In a Lockean liberal society, if certain individuals come to believe that they or their property are being harmed by poor air and water quality or by the degradation of other natural resources, they may appeal to government or to judges only insofar as they can show that their own lives and properties are threatened by the use that others are making of their lives and properties. To make a law or to have standing before the law, members of the political society have to show a life- or property-interest, which government exists to protect. There can be no prior "rights" belonging to the land, or the air, or the water, or the animals. Thus, environmental "interests" can arise only as the interests of particular members of society with regard to their lives and properties. No wonder that in a liberally minded society environmentalism can arise only as one interest among many in competition with other interests. And naturally, any discovery that a person's private property carries environmental value for others will have to be dealt with in a way that requires the government, by majority will, to compensate the property owner. As in the Pennsylvania case, protection of privately owned wetlands for public environmental purposes will require that government satisfy the property owner by buying out (or compensating for) the interest that government wants to protect. If government cannot obtain either a majority legislative vote to make a more drastic legal change or a sufficient amount of funding (through tax collection or user fee) to compensate the land owner, then, government has no authority to act on behalf of a public interest, which, by definition, does not exist.[5]

The point here is not that good environmental laws can never be written or enforced, but rather that, on Lockean liberal grounds, the soundness of the environment cannot be considered a fundamental obligation of government prior to the legislative and adjudicatory processes that exist to protect individual liberty and private properties. Consequently, ecological well-being has to prove its importance by having a legislative advocate with an environmental interest or claim who can deliver sufficient evidence to convince a majority of legislators that such an interest really belongs to each of them and to those they represent. But this will have to be done time and again, in case after case, and not once and for all, because government's mandate always comes back to the protection of private property and liberty, not to the protection of ecological sustainability as a precondition of private property and liberty.

Let's return now to Locke's statement that one's right to one's own possessions "excludes the common right of other men," with one exception, namely, "at least where there is enough and as good left in common for others" (134). Doesn't this establish an important pre-political limit to autonomous possession and open the way to environmental laws that can assure "enough and as good" for others?

In fact, it does nothing of the kind. Locke's rule about the limits of individual appropriation has to do with the human condition in the state of nature, prior to the creation of civil government. The obligation, in that state of nature, to leave enough for others is a rule against waste, that is, a rule against taking more than one can use before it rots or degrades to uselessness. "As much as any one can make use of to any advantage of life before it spoils," says Locke, "so much he may by his labour fix a property in; whatever is beyond this is more than his share, and belongs to others. Nothing was made by God for man to spoil or destroy" (136). There is no hint here of a common responsibility for the ecological commons. This is a moral obligation for each individual.

However, once money is created and the rules of civil society are established, it becomes possible for individuals to acquire far more than they can use immediately, because money does not spoil. Money allows for greater accumulation and greater production to sell to others, and commerce multiplies goods and services for the greater good of everyone. The key to all of this is that money (capital) has no spoilage limit. So there is no limit to what one can store up, because money does not spoil like apples or nuts or cabbages. As Leo Strauss explains, "In civil society the right of appropriation is completely freed from the shackles by which it was still fettered under Locke's original law of nature: the introduction of money has introduced 'larger possessions and a right to them'; man may now 'rightfully and without injury, possess more than he himself can make use of.'"[6] Individuals enter into society, according to Strauss's explanation of Locke,

> in order not so much to preserve as to enlarge their possessions. The property which is to be "preserved" by civil society is not "static" property—the small

farm which one has inherited from one's fathers and which one will hand down to one's children—but "dynamic" property. . . . Civil society merely creates the conditions under which the individuals can pursue their productive-acquisitive activity without obstruction.[7]

The natural law of a spoilage limit is not a civil law and it holds only for individuals in the state of nature. Civil law is written and enforced to protect individual lives and properties. There is no natural law that obligates governments, over against individuals, to keep the ecological commons from being used up or wasted.

Breaking Locke's Hold on the Commons

If, in contrast to Locke and liberalism, we want to argue that the ecological context of society should be given foundational consideration and not only secondary consideration in public law, then we need to find a different point of departure. If the natural environment—a vast array of diversified creatures with their own identities and glories—is part of God's creation, then this fact, along with human labor, needs to be taken into account when we consider the responsibilities God has given humans. And, in fact, that is precisely what the biblical story—slighted by Locke—does. From the first pages of the Bible we learn of God's commission to humans—the image of God—to "work [the garden] and *take care of it*" (Gen. 2:15). Humans bear an obligation to God to care for the garden, not a right to take possession of whatever part of it they choose when they mix their labor with it. Furthermore, when God gives commandments for human flourishing on earth, the sabbath principle is central: "Six days you shall labor and do all your work, but the seventh day is a Sabbath to the Lord your God. On it you shall not do any work, neither you, nor your son or daughter, nor your manservant or maidservant, nor your animals, nor the alien within your gates" (Ex. 20:9–10). Human labor, from the biblical point of view, is not an extension of each person's self-possession but rather an expression of human responsibility to God under creation-wide conditions. In other words, the possessions of any Israelite have attached to them a stewardship requirement, namely, that everyone, *even the animals*, must rest every seventh day. God does not command the owner—predicated on the fact of his ownership—to allow his animals and his servants to rest, as if the decision to grant rest comes from the owner to his possessions. No, God is the one who directly commands the day of rest for every creature.

Consequently, the owner's "possessions" carry with them a condition: no work for either humans or animals on the sabbath. All of this is part of the biblical message that no one has absolute possession of anything, even of oneself. God is the owner of all things; humans are only stewards of what belongs ultimately to God. Locke's individual grounds his possessiveness in the natural law of freedom and self-possession. For Locke, the individual is "absolute lord of his own person and possessions" (184). On biblical grounds, by contrast, individuals remain responsible to the God who possesses them and sets the conditions for the care of creation. They are absolute lords of nothing, not of themselves and not of their possessions.[8]

When God gives Israel more elaborate commandments about responsibility for the land of promise they are about to enter, the sabbath principle is extended. Not only humans and animals must rest; the land itself must rest. "When you enter the land I am going to give you," says the Lord, "the land itself must observe a sabbath to the Lord. For six years sow your fields, and for six years prune your vineyards and gather their crops. But in the seventh year the land is to have a sabbath of rest, a sabbath to the Lord. Do not sow your fields or prune your vineyards. Do not reap what grows of itself or harvest the grapes of your vineyards" (Lev. 25:2–5). The pattern of rest here was built in as an encumbrance, a stewardship obligation, from the outset, as a precondition of human community. Calvin DeWitt sees the sabbath principle as one of three basic ecological principles articulated in the Bible. The other two are earthkeeping and fruitfulness. To keep the earth (Gen. 3:15) means to "make sure that the creatures under our care are maintained with all their proper connections." To heed the fruitfulness principle means that humans may eat and use the earth's fruits but must not destroy its ability to continue to be fruitful.[9]

This is all part of the biblical story that Locke ignored when he gave us his own creation account. Locke's god simply turns over the world to autonomous individuals for their individual appropriation. Locke's creatures have nothing to fear except the potentially violent claims of other autonomous individuals. Each is a steward of nothing; each is, instead, absolute lord of his own possessions, defined as that with which one has mixed one's labors. For biblical Israel, by contrast, humans must above all fear the Lord who gives life and holds humans accountable for the way they exercise their stewardship of God's creation, including the animals and the land. And God speaks to Israel not as a collection of self-possessing individuals but as a community with a common land, common responsibilities, and a law that has the sabbath principle built right into it.

Most Americans now recognize intuitively, if not in a critical and reflective way, that human freedom and use of different kinds of property cannot flourish or be sustained for future generations unless justice is done to water, air, land, plants, and animals. The environmental movement has been built on that intuitive insight, which grows as people become dissatisfied with polluted air and water. Nevertheless, the dominant influence of liberal ideology in our political tradition guides our approach to environmental protection, which becomes one cause among many in a system that begins and ends with individual freedom.

However, justice for both people and the nonhuman world demands that we seek a different approach to politics and the law. Justice requires a change at the foundations and not only at the level of lobbying tactics. Given our present system and dominant ideology, this will mean some very hard-fought battles to be sure. But what we need is not merely a few more government regulations or a little more federal expenditure here and there to satisfy environmentalists. We need a fundamentally different perspective on *government's* responsibility for the well-being of the commons, a perspective that arises from the full biblical picture of human responsibility rather than from Locke's "creation" story.[10]

The Constitutional Crisis over Slavery

Those who are naively optimistic that Americans will not suffer a governing crisis over environmental concerns should take another look at the constitutional crisis we faced over slavery. The fundamental injustice of slavery was incorporated into the federal Constitution of the new United States of America from the outset on largely Lockean grounds. State governments existed to protect the lives and properties of those recognized as legitimately able to possess property. The federal government was then created as a qualified and limited grant of power from the states, which were seen as the original civil governments. Just as the states had no authority to take away private property but only to protect it, since individual self-government was more original than the states, so the federal government had no authority to dislodge or displace state governments but only to protect them. In the federal Constitution and the constitutions of slave states, slaves had an ambiguous identity as both persons and the property of slave owners. Without a majority vote in any state legislature to change its constitutional system, slavery could not be overturned, because government existed to protect private property, including the owner's property in slaves. And of course the federal government had no authority to change the constitutional system of any state.

Tragically, this two-level constitutional injustice was not redressed without a civil war, which revealed the breakdown, not the success, of American republican government. The federal union became ungovernable. The point is that if a large majority of people does not rise up to address a fundamental, constitutional injustice by amending the Constitution, the crisis of governance can occur at a very deep level indeed—even producing civil war. After the Civil War, constitutional amendments essentially removed black people from the list of "things" that other people could own as property and gave the federal courts and government greater authority over some legal matters originally held by the states. What became clear is that constitutional justice could not be done to black people as long as their interests were taken into consideration only as the disputed property claims of autonomously free white property owners. The law had to change in a fundamental way and not merely at the level of statute law.

Think how inadequate and unjust it would have been if instead of abolishing slavery, either by peaceful means or by war, Congress and the courts had merely tried to ameliorate the conditions of slavery by interest-group pressures. Imagine an interest group lobbying for better treatment of slaves and pushing Congress to fund a few benefits for slaves. The benefits could have been regulations restraining the owner's punishment of slaves or requiring that slave families not be broken up, or they could have been funding a social-security provision for older slaves after they were no longer productive on the plantations. Of course, these hypothetical regulations and benefits would never have made it through Congress without overcoming the resistance of lobbyists for the slave owners. Such regulations and benefits, the opponents would have said, would only increase taxes, establish a new federal bureaucracy, increase the cost of production, and illegitimately interfere with the rights of property owners and with the rights of the states to govern themselves. Moreover, the regulations and benefits would never be permanent, because a subsequent change in the control of Congress or a shift in popular opinion might lead to the reversal or weakening of those laws. Today, we recognize that all the lobbying in the world to assist slaves would never have achieved justice within the slave system. The injustice existed at the root, at the constitutional foundation of slavery. The whole system had to go. Slavery had to be rejected entirely. Black people are people and must be recognized as having the same pre-political rights as all other humans.

The analogy I want to draw between the end of slavery and protection of the environment is simply that the environment must be taken into consideration at a constitutional level. I am not equating black people with the nonhuman environment, nor am I suggesting that a constitutional amendment could solve all environmental problems once and for all. There are many ways in which the two realities are not analogous. But just as we now recognize that black people, like white people, deserve equal treatment under the law, with a right to speak, assemble, and practice their religions, so we should recognize that environmental well-being is something that should be protected at the foundation of the political order and not simply as an outcome of politics. Or to say it another way, the rights to assemble, to speak, and to practice one's religion freely, for example, are not politically negotiable interests but constitutional preconditions of politics and government. This, I am arguing, should also be the case for environmental protection.

Of course, some aspects of environmental health and well-being cannot become known until social development, productivity, commerce, and scientific advances make us aware of ecological limits and threats to the environment. But it would make a great difference if environmental conditions triggered an inescapable, constitutional requirement for government to act rather than merely stirring up environmental interest groups to press their interests before Congress. The former would mean that environmental protection would be considered a fundamental requirement. The latter means that environmental protection is legitimate only when the legislative process can justify government's interference in the more basic reality of autonomous individuals doing what they want with their lives and properties.

The overturning of slavery demonstrated that the first principle of public justice cannot be individual freedom and property rights. The first principle must be the proper recognition and identification in law of every person and nonhuman entity so that each can be given its due. And the precondition for this first principle is that a constitutionally established government must be held accountable to uphold public justice in accord with the constitutional preconditions on which it is established. The rights of individuals, including their property rights, in other words, should be set in the context, on the foundation, of justice being done to the full meaning of persons, institutions, and the nonhuman environment in which human life is possible and sustainable.

If, as history unfolds, people in a society discover that an earlier law misidentified or failed to do justice to the true character of a person, or institution, or natural thing, then the revision of the law has to be a priority. To be sure, it would have been wonderful if slavery could have been brought to an end amicably by peaceful constitutional revision, by substantial and long-term public investment in the education, job training, healthcare, and property ownership of newly freed slaves, and by helping slave owners make a transition from the old economic system to a new one. But absent a peaceful transition, surely the liberation of slaves and the revision of the Constitution to recognize them as people had to take precedence over the economic compensation of slave owners for their loss of "property."

This is not to suggest that in the case of legislative decisions to protect wetlands, for example, compensation need never be considered for those who were earlier granted the right to own the land without any environmental encumbrances. The expropriation of property by eminent domain, as another example, should, in accord with principles of justice, take into account the investment of the property owner and offer compensation. Yet the justice of compensation should not be determined solely by the private property rights and potential future value of the land to the owner under market conditions that ignore long-term ecological well-being.[11] To the contrary, even the assessment of just compensation should be determined by reference to the wider context of environmental sustainability, the ecological and public well-being of the wider community and future generations, the public costs of achieving that well-being, and the injustice of earlier laws that ignored all such considerations.

Stewardship as Precondition

What we need, in other words, is a reconceptualization of public justice for the environment. Important fundamentals of environmental protection need to be part of the basic law and not merely the occasional outcome of congressional and state legislation. Protection of ecological health, as one of the preconditions of all public and market relations, should become as fundamental as the protection of civil rights for individuals. With respect to land and other parts of the natural world this would require the continuing public-legal clarification of distinctions such as those between forest lands, wetlands, and agricultural land.

Environmental protection might best be thought of as a stewardship obligation for any owner or user similar to the way zoning works in a town or city. Homeowners and business owners do not gain unqualified private-property rights to the land and resources they "own" and use. Homeowners in my town may not set up a commercial or industrial business on property zoned for residences. They may not burn trash in their backyards. They may sell their property, but only with the public encumbrances attached to it. And so forth. Land zoned for business or industry is encumbered with special obligations. The simple fact is that land ownership is encumbered with stewardship obligations from the start. That which can be negotiated and changed over time through ordinary legislation includes changing the borders of differently zoned land, altering the tax rates for different kinds of properties, and adjusting the stringency of certain zoning requirements. But the fact of zoning for the good of the commons—the fact of stewardship obligations built into any privately owned property—is there to stay. In certain respects and in some places, environmental protection now has the status of a fundamental encumbrance, not subject to annual legislative or executive change. Certain clean air and water standards, or wetland zonings, or land and water uses are now standard and basic. But most of these achievements have been won by legislation arising from interest-group pressures and negotiations that have not changed the liberal mind-set that led to the achievement.

Robert Nelson credits Chicago economist Frank Knight with having done more than any other American economist to call into question the "progressive gospel" of modern liberal economics, which Nelson believes has become the dominant American religion. Over the years, writes Nelson, the Chicago school of economists opposed the progressive vision of scientific management of the economy (and thereby much of society), but the Chicago school "has typically defended the basic values of material progress and economic efficiency."[12] Knight was the lone exception, says Nelson, because Knight "also doubted the possibilities for any improvement in the human condition based on material progress. He rejected the prevailing euphoria with respect to science, including the efforts of the economics profession to develop in a scientific mode" (326). This is one of the reasons Knight became sympathetic with the concerns of environmentalists. He helped show that the emerging environmental crises are related to the crisis of optimistic progressive economics and thus to the crisis of American governance, all three of which have deep religious roots. "It follows," then, says Nelson, "that the legitimacy of American government in the twenty-first century is likely to require some new governing vision" (327).

Indeed, the need for a "new governing vision" is precisely why I am urging consideration of a Christian-democratic approach to politics. The public order—the republic—of which we are a part needs to be understood as something more than the extension of self-government by self-possessing individuals who ordain government only to protect their lives and properties. What is needed is a new mind-set—a new public-justice orientation—that starts with the covenanted character of society and of the political community itself.

CHAPTER EIGHT

Citizenship and Electoral Reform

To be a citizen is to be a member of a political community or state. A political community is constituted by citizens subject to government, both of which should be subject to the law. Precisely because government has authority to enforce the laws on citizens, citizens ought to have a say in framing the laws. Therefore, a just state requires representation of its citizens in the lawmaking body of government. This little four-sentence argument took centuries of contention and conflict—some of it violent warfare—to be realized in practice. Democratic, representative government in a constitutional state is a very precious prize indeed.

A presupposition of my argument for representative government is that citizens and government constitute a political community. In other words, a commitment to the realization of a just political community is the necessary presupposition of the responsibilities of citizenship and government. To talk of teachers and students presupposes a school. To talk of employers and employees presupposes a business enterprise. To talk of parents and children presupposes a family. Likewise, to talk of citizens and government presupposes the kind of institutional responsibilities people exercise in a political community, distinct from the responsibilities they exercise as family members, church members, school members, and so forth.

One of the weaknesses of the American republic, however, is the weakness of its commitment to building a political community. The reasons for this are both structural and ideological. Structurally, the United States was organized as a federation, which was agreed to only reluctantly after an attempt at an even weaker confederation failed. The real centers of gravity for political community at the American founding were the states, not the federation. Even our language conveys this fact. We call New York and Illinois and the other 48 entities in our union, "states." We do not typically refer to the United States as our "state," for it is a *federation* of states, thus "The United States (plural) of America." Structurally, as the U.S. Constitution makes clear, the several states are the original units of governing authority, the real political communities in which citizens have direct representation in state legislatures. The several states are the creators of the federal government, having granted it only limited authority to exercise only a few common functions on behalf of them all. Those functions are chiefly the regulation of interstate commerce and the provision of defense against foreign attack. As for the structure of representation in Congress, it is clear that the states, not their citizens, established the framework for federal representation. From the beginning, there was to be no direct, nationwide representation of citizens in the federal Congress or the presidency. Citizens would elect representatives and senators from their states to go to Washington, and an electoral college of state delegates would elect the president of the United States. To this day, even with reforms that now allow for direct election of senators and (almost) of the president, there is still no arrangement for nationwide representation of American citizens in Congress.

There have, however, been major structural changes in the federal union since the founding. The most significant change occurred as a result of the Civil War. When the North defeated the South, the federal government essentially redefined the federal union, giving it an authority over states that was not anticipated in the beginning. Not only were the slaves emancipated and the plantation economy of the South destroyed, but new amendments to the Constitution gave the federal courts and Congress an authority to govern all American citizens directly in ways that earlier would have been rejected as an illegitimate interference of the federal government in the sovereignty of the states. The second major structural change emerged from the Great Depression and World War II, as the federal government established more and more social and economic programs for the nation as a whole. Today, the reality of a nationwide political community is self-evident. Americans are more significantly citizens of the United States than they are citizens of the states in which they happen to live. Yet, the structure of the system of representation has not changed to accommodate the new reality of a national political community. There is still no nationwide representation of citizens in Congress. This is why the fashioning of federal legislation is accomplished by a bargaining process among representatives and senators from the states, who often cooperate to look after regional interests (such as agriculture), as they spend most of their time brokering the demands of national interest groups. The people in their role as citizens of the national political community (in contrast to their role in national interest-groups) have no means of being represented in the conduct and outcome of congressional legislation.

The second reason for a weak American political community is the dominance of liberal ideology (whether in its conservative or liberal version) among citizens. From a liberal point of view, as we discussed in earlier chapters, humans are not political by nature; they are not made for political community. By nature, humans are idealized as free and independent individuals. For the protection of life and property, however, individuals agree to establish a common government, and their contract establishes a "civil society," as John Locke called it. Yet even when liberals recognize that citizens and government constitute a "civil society," they do not arrive at a normative idea of what the political community, as such, should be. That is because government exists, from a liberal point of view, only to protect and enhance the life of individuals. The state or political community has no identity of its own, no normative purpose to realize as a community of public justice. Therefore, even the purpose of representation in the lawmaking body of the state is to make sure that individual interests are taken into account and that the executive government is held in check and restrained from trying to become more than it should be. For this reason, most citizens do not have a strong sense of civic responsibility for the well-being of either their particular state or the national political community. In fact, for many, government, including Congress, is suspect as a potential drain on (or threat to) individual freedom, property, and income. Consequently, most Americans, as citizens of the nation, are not conscious of their lack of adequate representation in Congress.

If we keep in mind both the structural and ideological reasons for a weak sense of political community in the United States, it will help us see why our system of electoral representation serves citizens so poorly today. The aim of this chapter is to explain why our present electoral system is deficient and to make the case for a reform of the system that addresses the structural weakness just mentioned. The reform proposed cannot in itself bring about a change of mind among those committed to a liberal ideology. But it will become evident both in my criticism of the existing electoral system and in my proposal for a better one how the argument arises from a Christian-democratic point of view, which envisions an open public square in which all citizens have opportunity for equal participation and direct representation.

The Electoral System Today

The American system of electoral representation was designed to facilitate the realization of a majority governing consensus at the federal level, based on adequate representation of the states of the union. House and Senate electoral campaigns culminate in voting—a process carried out in single-member electoral districts in the states (either House districts or the state as a whole for Senate races) where, by majority vote, one candidate is chosen to represent everyone in the voting district. A majority (or plurality) vote determines the win; the winner takes all. Those who vote against the winner are not considered to be unrepresented after the election but rather are recognized to be represented by the winner. To accept this system willingly and happily, citizens must agree that the majority vote in each district expresses the true will of the whole body of citizens in that district. Or to put it negatively, minority political viewpoints are not supposed to be represented. Citizens who have minority opinions deserve the same protection that other parochial opinions deserve, namely, the right of free expression outside the legislative process. Those with minority views can come back again at the next election and try to convince more voters so that they might become the majority winners and represent everyone. But inside the legislative process, after the election is over, it is the majority winners from all of the voting districts in the several states who should have free reign to work out the one will of the body politic as a whole. Political debate during election campaigns, therefore, has to be oriented toward winning a majority vote in a given district. Winning a majority, or in some cases a plurality, of the vote is what authorizes a representative to enter Congress on behalf of everyone in the winner's House or Senate voting district.

But now, this question: what if American citizens do not, in fact, constitute a homogeneous political mass that can be adequately represented by simple majority winners in single-member districts? What if the diverse political views of citizens cannot be condensed into a single, majority viewpoint, especially when electoral majorities appear increasingly to lack strong definition? The United States is, to be sure, a single republic, but what if its citizens differ significantly in their views of how the republic as a whole should be governed, as happens to be true of libertarians, socialists, egalitarian liberals, moral conservatives, greens, neoconservatives, and others? In this case, does it make sense to have an electoral system that forces citizens to seek a simple majoritarian electoral conclusion?

If one's view of political life and one's concern for a sound program of national government are grounded in a worldview different from the worldviews of other citizens, how can one feel satisfied with an electoral process that frustrates one's desire to engage in serious public debate from that point of view? Could it be that the American electoral system has become as ill-suited to a culturally and religiously diverse, nationally integrated society as the current public school system is ill-suited to that same society? Is there not a better way to structure the electoral process in order to make possible serious public debate and real national representation for our diverse citizenry?

Assessing the Problems

Because of an unhealthy takeover by media, money, and marketing, says W. Lance Bennett, Americans now find themselves being manipulated by an electoral system that no longer provides for meaningful representation. We have entered an era "in which electoral choices are of little consequence because an electoral system in disarray can generate neither the party unity nor the levels of public agreement necessary to forge a winning and effective political coalition."[1]

The goal of our republic, argues George F. Will, should be "deliberative democracy through representatives who function at a constitutional distance from the people."[2] Today, however, we no longer have "an ethic, or a political philosophy, or a constitutional doctrine that encourages people to distinguish between licit and illicit advantages from government."[3] To the contrary, "the problem is the everydayness of, the routinization of, the banality of the process by which private interests methodically seek to bend public power to private purposes."[4]

These statements, along with dozens of others that could be added, point to a problem of complex proportions. The evidence suggests that numerous interconnected aspects of our political system are implicated in a diffuse crisis. It is not merely campaign-finance laws, or interest-group pressures, or career incumbency that can be singled out as the sole culprit. These along with many other aspects of our electoral and governance systems appear to be linked together in an intricate web of declining civic confidence, electoral apathy or antipathy, and governmental disorder. There appears to be an intensifying incongruity between our expanding, highly mobile, multicultural, *national* population, on the one hand, and the means by which that population is formally represented in Washington, on the other. There is an

expanding gap between the decreasing significance of national elections
and the growing power of unrepresentative interest groups. The need for
Congress and the president to act responsibly on behalf of the country as a
whole is thwarted by a system that allows less and less room for public deliberation about the common good, about the broad national interest.
Strengthening deliberative democracy, building confidence in government,
and achieving meaningful representation can come about, it would seem,
only if Americans can make changes that will systematically and simultaneously alter many aspects of the political system.

There are at least six components of our electoral system that now appear
to be aggravating one another in a downward spiral that threatens to undermine the governance of the country.

1. Our huge country of more than 250 million people has only a single,
   elected, nationwide official—the president. Even though the Congress
   as a whole is co-responsible for federal governance, no senator or representative is elected nationwide with a responsibility to serve the
   common good of the country as a whole. James L. Sundquist, a senior
   fellow emeritus of The Brookings Institution, explains that since all
   members of Congress are elected by districts, "Congress as a whole is
   not accountable to the people as a whole. Each voter can act to throw
   out one rascal, but the others are beyond reach. . . . Thus the Congress
   is in a very real sense an irresponsible body, beyond control by the voters, whatever their mood."[5]

2. National political parties, which function primarily in connection with
   presidential campaigns, are almost powerless to mold national agendas
   that can bind elected officials together in their respective parties for
   governance after an election. The party structures that exist perform a
   very small percentage of the work necessary for meaningful representation in a modern democracy. Today's political parties, says Will, are
   "mere money-raising and money-distributing operations, and not even
   the most important raisers and disbursers."[6] "Running for Congress is
   today an activity akin to pure entrepreneurship on the part of candidates who put themselves forward. They find a market (a district) and
   a market niche (a potential majority to be cobbled together from various factions); they merchandise themselves with advertising paid for by
   venture capitalists (contributors) who invest in candidates."[7] Our political parties as they now function are unable to hold elected party
   members accountable as disciplined teams to govern in accord with
   campaign platforms and promises.[8]

3. Individuals who win elections in our system each represent a voting district rather than a constituency that belongs to the same party as the winning candidate. This means that as many as half or more of the voters (along with many who do not vote) end up being "represented" by individuals they wish were not representing them. That is to say, many voters have as their official representative the candidate they actually voted against. Thus, the already weak link between citizens and their elected officials is further weakened by the decidedly antipathetic attitude of some citizens toward their members of Congress. Moreover, evidence suggests that this antipathy is easily transferred to government as a whole and is not confined to particular representatives.[9]

4. Most voters have so little positive connection with those who supposedly represent them that they feel alienated from (and often antipathetic toward) the political process generally. In fact, in federal elections over the past few decades, close to 50 percent of the eligible voters have not bothered to vote. Even among those who have voted, most know little about the officeholder who represents the district in which they live. "Most Americans today," says Bennett, "experience elections as empty rituals that offer little hope for political dialogue, genuine glimpses of candidate character, or the emergence of a binding consensus on where the nation is going and how it ought to get there."[10]

5. Elected representatives, identified with political parties that are too weak to hold them accountable and representing districts where half or more of the voters are apathetic or antipathetic, are officials who function essentially as lone rangers.[11] This is true both in the running of their campaigns as well as in the way they serve in elected office. This makes concerted congressional action on behalf of the nationwide public even more difficult to achieve. Elected representatives who are neither tied together by party discipline nor obligated by election mandates find that they must deal with other demands and pressures that are more forceful and direct, namely, the demands from organized interest groups.

6. The most influential political connections that the president and most senators and representatives have today are in fact with interest groups, not with national parties or supportive voters in their districts. This holds true both for the conduct of business in their elected offices as well as for the conduct of election campaigns and the fund-raising necessary for those campaigns. Will says that governments have always responded to interests, but today the word "respond" is far too benign to

capture the truth about political reality. "The modern state does not merely respond to interests, it generates them and even, in effect, organizes them."[12]

Considering these six interconnected components of the federal election and governing systems together, we can note at least two very profound and dire consequences. The first is that elected representatives now function more as interest-group brokers than as public-interest representatives or trustees of the national political community or commonwealth. This is the judgment that Bennett reaches in developing his criticism of campaign finance laws, the marketing of candidates, and the distorting connection between contemporary politics and the media. Individual candidates at all levels, he says, "have been separated from their party loyalties by an elaborate system of individual funding from interest groups. . . . There is precious little room left for thinking about—much less, acting on—any broader public interest."[13] Bennett continues,

> Celluloid candidates and imaginary issues are just the symptoms of deeper problems with the system. The weakening link between elections and governing is the more fundamental problem. . . . [T]he centrifugal pull of special interests at every level of government has left little chance for coherent action on pressing public problems. Simply enacting a national budget each year has become a major challenge and frequent crisis of governing.[14]

The second consequence is that most citizens who do choose to engage in civic action at the national level now put most of their time and money into the interest-group pressuring game, or they take off into protest movements, marches, and litigation in the courts. Less and less civic action materializes in the form of mature, public-interest debate during and after election campaigns among competing parties offering meaningful programs. The truth is that citizens are relatively powerless either to give clear mandates at election time or to hold individual representatives accountable once they enter office. Interest-group activism—beyond control of the political parties and of Congress—appears to most citizens to be the primary means of exercising political influence even though it is a means that almost never allows for a consideration of the law-making process from a public-interest viewpoint—that is, from a point of view concerned with the public good of the nation as a whole, with the common good of the entire republic.

Interest-group politics in turn increasingly squeezes Congress into the mold of an interest-group brokerage house, so that the republic is left without representative governance in the proper and full sense of that term. As Bennett puts it:

> The fragmentation of the governing system has at once produced a decline in broad, programmatic national policies and an increase of what might be called government in the trenches. Both on Capitol Hill and in the executive branch, committee and agency personnel are working overtime writing the rules and regulations that bring thousands of small fragmentary policies on line consistent with the interests of the groups that have pushed them into legislative and bureaucratic agendas. This flurry of micro politics belies any suggestion that government has ceased activity. Rather, government has become even more dedicated to the writing and rewriting of rules and regulations and haggling over where federal responsibilities lie for increasingly uncoordinated politics. The point is simply that government is less and less occupied with passing laws backed by the force of governing ideas.[15]

In sum, our predicament is this: Americans—as citizens of the nation—are not represented in a way that allows them to fulfill their public-interest responsibilities; parties are too weak to connect voters to those who win elections; and interest-group brokering has displaced public-interest statecrafting to the point where more and more citizens realize that the republic does not have an accountable government in Washington.

What Representation Should Mean

Before turning to recommendations for reform that might begin to address this complex network of problems, we must first ask what representative government should mean. Surely one of the first principles of a sound electoral system is that it should galvanize strong connections between citizens and their elected representatives. For this reason, the tie between political parties and citizens should be stronger than the tie between the lobbying interest groups and their members, because interest groups neither submit to elections nor come under widespread popular control. Parties, through which citizens organize themselves as citizens for elections and for governance, should have greater power in shaping national policy than should the groups that intentionally lobby for particular interests and not for the common good. Political parties should function as serious team builders, closely connecting the citizens who are their members with candidates for the Senate, the House, and the presidency so that candidates no longer run as freewheeling individuals and are no longer left to function chiefly as interest-group brokers once in office. Political parties should function as potent, public accountability structures, doing more than simply coordinating minor campaign tasks for lone-ranger candidates who remain dependent on extra-party campaign contributions. Parties should have to bear the burden of responsibility for devising platforms and programs with which to guide and discipline their candidates—platforms and programs that can be put to the test of public judgment in elections. Citizens, in other words, need to be able to hold candidates accountable as members of party teams both before and after elections.

Furthermore, in a highly mobile, multicultural, and ideologically diverse national society a sound electoral system ought to make possible the representation of real citizens rather than the representation of artificial and often absurdly gerrymandered voting districts. All voters, not simply the winning majorities in separate districts, should be able to see and feel the direct connection between their votes and those who represent them in Washington. The electoral system should be structured to invite rather than discourage voter participation. All voters should have the opportunity to get involved in the kind of civic debate and campaigning that can make a real difference at election time.

A workable system of representation, from this point of view, should also generate a greater number of national political leaders—members of the House and Senate who are recognized by people across the country as representing their point of view and their program goals for government. Civic debate that has real political significance should occur during electoral contests among national party leaders who represent party teams. These leaders, moreover, need to be accountable primarily to citizens through their parties rather than to interest groups.

In sum, American citizens should have an electoral system that allows all of them to be represented meaningfully, that encourages the growth of strong nationwide parties that connect voters and elected officials closely, and that elevates public-interest statecrafting above interest-group brokering as the chief task of government in Washington.

Pluralistic Reform of the Electoral System

The kind of electoral system devised by most democracies in the world is one that allows almost every vote to count, not just those of the majority, and one that puts the burden of governance on citizen-connected parties rather than on freewheeling interest-group brokers. It is called *proportional representation*, or PR for short.[16] While there are many ways to design an electoral system with greater or lesser degrees of PR, a good first step for the United States, that does not call for anything revolutionary, would be a reform that simply alters the method of electing members to our House of Representatives while leaving everything else about the Senate, the presidency, and the federal system intact.[17] Once this first step is taken, however, even if only in a few states, the consequences could gradually unfold constructively to touch each of the problems outlined above.[18]

Under current law, population determines the number of seats allotted to each state in the House of Representatives. For the entire country a numerical proportion is calculated between the number of House seats (435) and the total U.S. population. Each seat is supposed to represent the same number of people. Once that number is determined, each state knows how many representatives it may have, based on its population. Each state then carves up its territory into the number of districts corresponding to the number of House seats it may fill. Each of those districts then becomes a single-member election zone to be represented in Congress by the candidate who wins a majority (or plurality) of the votes cast in the election. Our system tends to eliminate all but two candidates in any district, and each of them battles just to get 51 percent of the vote in order to win everything. Each wants to appeal to as many voters as possible and to alienate as few as possible. Candidates who can appeal to only a minority of the population tend to be squeezed out of electoral contests.[19] Voter apathy and antipathy spring from the growing incongruity between the appearance that something significant is happening and the deeper reality that the election campaign's outcome is likely to be inconsequential.

In place of the present system, we should turn each state into a *single, multimember district* from which its allotted number of House seats would be filled by a means of PR. For example, if Illinois is allowed twenty-two seats in the House of Representatives, then under PR a variety of political parties could each run twenty-two candidates for the entire state in an election that would determine the winners by a proportional count. If the Democrats were to win 50 percent of the statewide vote, they would get eleven seats in the House, not more or less. If the Republicans were to win 35 percent of the vote, they would get eight seats in the House, not more or less. If the Green Party, the Libertarian Party, and the Rainbow Coalition were each to win 5 percent of the vote, then each would get one seat in the House, not more or less.

Not only would nearly every vote count in this PR system—with minority as well as majority parties gaining representation—but nearly every voter would be represented in the House by the party he or she actually votes for. All who vote Democrat, no matter where they live in the state, would be represented by the Democrat team. All who vote Republican would be represented by the Republican team. All who vote Green or Libertarian (or some other) would be represented by the party they actually vote for.

Here is the beginning of a real connection—of genuine accountability—between voters as citizens and the official representatives they elect. It also opens the way to other benefits. For example, PR allows groups of citizens, even small groups, to gain representation through the electoral process without in any way inhibiting a genuine majority—even a very large majority—from winning control of the House. Instead of citizens giving up at the start because they feel their votes will not count (since under the current system those votes often do not count), they will instead be motivated under PR to work together to organize parties that can try to win a percentage of the House seats at election time. They will not have to win a majority of votes in a single district in order to assure representation for themselves. They will, however, have to work together to develop meaningful principles and programs and good candidates sufficient to convince a sizable group of citizens to vote for their candidates.

Toward Greater Accountability in Washington

The core value of PR is to make genuine representation possible—to connect voters and elected officials together in an accountability structure that keeps attention focused on the public interest. Those who are elected by means of PR will be tied very closely to the citizens who are members of their party. No party is likely to put forward candidates at election time who have not come up through its ranks to stand for what the party stands for. Every candidate will be part of a party team that continues to function after as well as before the election. The party will continue to shape and direct its principles, its programs, and its representatives. Since each candidate who gets elected will represent his or her party, each will continue to be closely watched, guarded, and disciplined by that party. In this kind of framework, career politicians can be a boon rather than a threat to good government.

The way to bring about accountable, deliberative government is to make it possible for citizens both to deliberate seriously (directly as citizens and not merely as members of interest groups) and to hold accountable the representatives they elect for the purpose of continuing that deliberation in Congress. The PR reform suggested here will help to do that by forcing a change in the way parties actually develop and function. Parties in a PR system have to work to define themselves very precisely and clearly in contrast to one another. Under PR, victory is gained not by candidates trying to be all things to all people and therefore saying as little as possible about what they will do in office. Rather, representation is gained by parties only in proportion to the number of votes won, and no party is able to "take all" by winning only 51 percent of the votes. Voters are free to vote for what they really believe in rather than simply for the lesser of evils. Under PR, voters gain the opportunity to learn what they are voting for, and if they do not like what they see in one party, they can vote for another party or work to start a new one. No party will be able to benefit from being fuzzy and non-committal. PR for the House of Representatives would open the way to real electoral competition.

Furthermore, each party under the new system would be pushed to define what it plans to do on a wide range of national concerns. It would have to show why its program and platform are best for the country on a large number of issues. Some citizens, interested in only one issue, may of course try to organize a party around that single issue, but over time, relatively few voters will cast their ballots for a party whose candidates refuse to address all the issues on which representatives are authorized to legislate in Congress. It will be too easy for another more comprehensive party to co-opt that issue and thus to marginalize or eliminate single-issue parties. If interest groups want to exercise influence in the political arena, they will have to deal with citizens from the start, at the grass-roots level where citizens are defining and organizing their parties. Interest groups will no longer be able to buy up candidates individually before elections or wait until after the election to pressure representatives individually when they arrive in Washington. Citizens, in other words, would be able under PR to take charge of their representatives from start to finish and thereby deal with various interest-group pressures both prior to and following elections. Disciplined parties would have no reason to send lone rangers to Washington to become interest-group brokers outside party control.

This is the only fundamental way to get at current problems associated with campaign financing and interest-group control over candidates and representatives. All other measures will only be stopgaps. As long as citizens have no direct way to support the representatives in whom they wish to place their confidence they will feel powerless to hold accountable those who do win elections. Under such circumstances, nothing can be done to control interest groups that are able to forge a close connection between their members and their leaders.[20] Only by putting real civic and electoral authority in the hands of citizens who are thereby able to hold representatives directly accountable will it be possible to subordinate private interest groups to the civic work of shaping law in the public interest for the common good.

The Emergence of National Parties

Once the conduct of elections shifts from the buying and selling of individual candidates to campaign debates among disciplined parties with clearly articulated legislative agendas, voters will become more involved in learning to judge among different party programs. With respect to a national legislative agenda, each party will want to maximize its strength nationwide. Representatives from the Republican Party in Illinois, for example, will need to work closely with Republicans from other states right from the start, not just after their elected representatives arrive in Washington. In fact, the initiative for organizing parties and party programs will most likely gravitate to the national level.[21] Democratic, Republican, and other parties will organize nationally and begin to map out consistent and coherent strategies for their House campaigns in each state. Integral, comprehensive, and distinctive programs will be developed by each national party and then put before the electorate by the branches of that party in each state as the parties campaign under PR for House seats. Any party that can demonstrate nationwide coherence and strength will have an advantage over parties that cannot demonstrate that capability.

One consequence of the emergence of national parties will be the appearance of a greater number of national political leaders. Each party will, in essence, put forward its best people for election. The most outstanding leaders of each party will, of course, have to win election in particular states. If one of the leaders of the Democrats happens to reside in Illinois, he or she will be able to enter Congress only by winning a seat in that state. But clearly that leader and others who win seats as Democrats across the country will become national leaders representing, to some extent, everyone who is a member of, or who votes for, the Democratic Party.

Additional consequences that are likely to follow from the formation of national parties and from the rise of national political leaders will include a more thorough apprenticeship for future candidates, the recruitment of a greater number of "statecrafters" into parties with comprehensive agendas, and a deepening of experience on the part of ordinary citizens who learn to practice real political teamwork over time. Under the new system, parties will have a tough time surviving if they limit themselves to raising money at election time for empty and meaningless campaigns of a few individuals who have loosely chosen that party's label for themselves. Instead, parties will have to begin doing the remaining 90 percent of the hard work that mature political parties must do, namely, educating and recruiting members; training and keeping close tabs on leaders; developing serious platforms and programs;

doing policy research; working as teams to clarify the distinctive contributions of their party's program in contrast to other party programs; and conducting ongoing coalition efforts with other parties where ideas and programs overlap or coincide.

Once the benefits of PR in the House begin to show themselves, the door will also open to another significant, even though modest reform, this one in the election of the president. Here I would propose a two-stage runoff system for the presidential election. The first stage would allow all eligible parties to put a presidential candidate on the ballot and there would be a first round of voting. If in the first round, one candidate were to win a majority of the votes, there would be no need for a second stage. However, if no candidate were to win a majority of the votes at the first stage, then a second stage would follow with a runoff election between the top two vote-getters in the first round. The winner of the second round of voting would then become president.

This system has the advantage of allowing voters to vote their conscience in the first round. They will not waste their vote by voting for the candidate they really believe in, even if they suspect that their first choice will not come out on top in the end. They do not have to limit themselves to choosing between the lesser of two evils. The number of votes received even by minor candidates in the first round can have a big impact on the thinking of the candidate who finally wins the presidency, as happened when Ross Perot won 19 percent of the vote in the 1992 presidential election. First-round votes will send important signals. The first round will allow parties with representatives in the House to put their national agenda before the public through their presidential candidate. At the same time, the certainty of arriving at an electoral conclusion at the end of the second stage means that consideration of a wide variety of candidates at the first stage will not create instability in the system.

Criticism of Proportional Representation

An argument for proportional representation faces at least two criticisms. The first is the charge that too many parties might come into existence and thus cause governmental instability if no party is able to gain majority control of the House. The second criticism is that a statewide slate of party representatives would not guarantee voters a personal representative close to home—from the particular district in which they live. Let's consider each of these criticisms.

In the first place, a greater number of parties may be precisely what the country needs if the diversity of its citizens is greater than can be represented by a superficial majority in a two-party system. Would it not be better, in other words, for Americans to be able to see in Congress exactly how diverse the body politic is rather than being misled by the impression that the Democrats and Republicans adequately represent the entire body politic? More parties in a system that allows for better and truer representation might bring greater rather than less stability to our system because it would make for greater voter confidence in elected representatives and in the political system as a whole. The real question is whether the present system is any longer stable.

Second, we must be careful not to compare apples with oranges. A system of PR tends to create parties that are more disciplined and coherent, each with a definite program and philosophy. Even if six or eight parties gained significant representation in the House, and even if none of them held a majority of seats, the process of negotiation and accommodation among them would likely be less chaotic and more purposeful than under the current system. Why? At present, majority control of the House by the Republicans, for example, gives a superficial impression of coherent, one-party control. Yet given the nature of our undisciplined parties and the interest-group influence on individual committees and representatives, the process of negotiation typically involves far more than six or eight groups or camps.

In the third place, most countries that employ a system of PR typically fix as a threshold a certain percentage of votes that any party must win in order to gain representation. In other words, there is a relatively simple way to avoid the problem of subjecting the House to the onslaught of too many small parties. A typical threshold, for example, is five percent; that is, a party would have to win at least five percent of the vote in order to gain a seat.[22] Establishing a threshold like this would clearly inhibit the proliferation of parties. The proposal for PR just outlined compromises the principle of pure PR, in any case, regardless of whether a threshold is established, because it starts with the state borders that currently exist. In proposing, for historical reasons, to keep the state boundaries intact, my proposal recognizes that states with heavy population concentrations—such as New York and California—will have far greater potential for genuine PR than will states such as Montana and the Dakotas.

Fourth and finally, it is important to point out that evidence gathered over time from the experience of other democracies shows that PR by itself is not the cause of government instability.[23] Instability of government typically has more to do with the governing system than it does with the electoral system. I am not proposing to change the three-branch system of American federal government to a parliamentary system in which the executive is chosen by the winning party or by a coalition of parties in the parliament. As long as the American president is elected independently to head the government, then PR in the House will never leave the United States without a government.

As for the second criticism that PR denies citizens a personal and local representative in Washington, we must look carefully at what would be lost and gained in the change to a new system. One reason for criticizing the present system of single-member districts is that they have less and less meaning as actual localities of public, civic identity. Gerrymandered districts often take on such strange shapes that they mean nothing to the people who live in them apart from functioning to secure a winner-take-all representative who is available in Washington to perform "constituency services."[24] Yet the present system has drained away much of the original meaning of a "representative"—someone in whom fellow citizens can place their confidence to make laws in the public interest. To the extent that a serious diminution of the representative's public legislative role has occurred (as exhibited in loss of voter confidence and actual distrust of government), it is a very weak argument that tries to defend the present system on the grounds that it provides citizens with a particular person to perform constituency services for them in Washington.

How much better it would be if citizens in a state could have teams of representatives—party teams—in whom they have confidence serving them in Washington. These would be legislators with whom voters could identify more closely, sharing the same philosophy and legislative agenda. In other words, if the primary meaning of representation should be achieved by a system that allows voters to be connected closely to the House members of their chosen party, then a citizen would typically have more than one representative in the House from their party to serve them. The PR reform I've proposed would allow citizens to select statewide party teams, which would become part of national party teams, rather than only a single, local representative. Thus, it would finally become possible for citizens to gain the thing most lacking in our current system, namely, national parties that directly represent the convictions of citizens about the governance of the country as a whole.

It must also be said that there are electoral systems, such as the one currently operative in Germany, that combine elements of both proportional and district representation.[25] If PR for our House of Representatives were to be introduced, as I've proposed, within the confines of present state borders and if the electoral system for Senate seats is left untouched, then we would retain ample representation of the most important traditional districts in our system, namely, the states. The need now is to build strong national parties and at the same time to make it possible for a diverse citizenry to gain genuine representation through publicly significant elections.[26]

Conclusion

Under the electoral system proposed here Americans would, in all probability, witness the rise of a variety of strong national parties serving to represent nearly every voter (and not just voting districts) in Congress. A greater number of national leaders, working with party teams, would give all citizens a voice in political debate. Interest-group politics could gradually be demoted to second place behind genuine party politics. And citizens could begin to experience real and direct representation in a more deliberative Congress. In all probability voter turnout would increase, and the demand for statecrafting could grow in strength as inter-party negotiations and accommodations begin to displace interest-group brokering in Congress. By means of such a system, the unity of the national political community would be reconciled with the representation of the true diversity of the nationwide citizenry. The pluralism of political convictions would be respected and channeled through real competition into shared responsibility for the political community—the national commonwealth that belongs to all citizens.

A just political community requires not only the legal recognition and protection of individual rights and nongovernment organizations. It also requires just ordering of the electoral system through which citizens are able to hold government accountable and gain representation in the legislative chamber. A Christian-democratic approach emphasizes the importance of the political community as much as it does the importance of the diversity of institutions, organizations, and viewpoints that should be protected by public laws. It does not aim for strong national unity at the expense of diversity, nor for freedom and diversity at the expense of a just *unum*—a just polity or commons shared by all citizens. Rather, it aims for a strong political community of citizens and government that can thereby do justice to the diverse associations, institutions, and responsibilities that belong to people who are always more than citizens.

Notes

Chapter 1

1. Robert P. Kraynak, *Christian Faith and Modern Democracy: God and Politics in the Fallen World* (Notre Dame, Ind.: University of Notre Dame Press, 2001), 1.

2. For an introduction to Christian democracy, see Michael P. Fogarty, *Christian Democracy in Western Europe: 1820–1953* (Westport, Conn.: Greenwood Press, 1974, 1957); Fogarty, *Phoenix or Cheshire Cat? Christian Democracy Past, Present, and Future* (London: Movement for Christian Democracy, 1996); Thomas Kselman and Joseph A. Buttigieg, eds., *European Christian Democracy: Historical Legacies and Comparative Perspectives* (Notre Dame, Ind.: University of Notre Dame Press, 2003); David Hanley, ed., *Christian Democracy in Europe: A Comparative Perspective* (London: Pinter, 1994); Hans Maier, *Revolution and Church: The Early History of Christian Democracy: 1789–1901*, trans. Emily M. Schossberger (Notre Dame, Ind.: University of Notre Dame Press, 1969); Roberto Papini, *Christian Democrat International*, trans. Robert Royal (Lanham, Md.: Rowman and Littlefield, 1996); John Witte Jr., ed. *Christianity and Democracy in Global Context* (Boulder, Colo.: Westview Press, 1993). For developments elsewhere, see John W. De Gruchy, *Christianity and Democracy* (Cambridge: Cambridge University Press, 1995); Gustavo Gutierrez, *A Theology of Liberation* (Maryknoll, N.Y.: Orbis Books, 1973); Jose Miguez Bonino, *Toward a Christian Political Ethics* (Philadelphia: Fortress Press, 1983); and Paul E. Sigmund, *Liberation Theology at the Crossroads: Democracy or Revolution?* (New York: Oxford University Press, 1990). On some of the contemporary developments across the "southern" part of the world, see Paul Freston, *Evangelicals and Politics in Asia, Africa, and Latin America* (Cambridge: Cambridge University Press, 2001).

3. See Perez Zagorin, *How the Idea of Religious Toleration Came to the West* (Princeton, N.J.: Princeton University Press, 2003); De Gruchy, *Christianity and Democracy*, 55–89; Jose Casanova, *Public Religions in the Modern World* (Chicago: University of Chicago Press, 1994), 11–39; and Martin Van Creveld, *The Rise and Decline of the State* (Cambridge: Cambridge University Press, 1999), 59–125.

4. Jeffrey Rosen, "Is Nothing Secular?" *New York Times Magazine*, 30 January 2000, 45.

5. Mark A. Noll, *America's God: From Jonathan Edwards to Abraham Lincoln* (New York: Oxford University Press, 2002), 53–92. See also De Gruchy, *Christianity and Democracy*, 84–94.

6. Noll, *America's God*, 367–401.

7. Maier, *Revolution*, 68–141; Christopher Dawson, *The Gods of Revolution: An Analysis of the French Revolution* (New York: Minerva Press, 1972); G. Groen van Prinsterer, "Unbelief and Revolution" (1847), in Harry Van Dyke, *Groen van Prinsterer's Lectures on Unbelief and Revolution* (Jordan Station, Ontario: Wedge Publishing Foundation, 1989), 293–539.

8. In addition to the literature cited in notes 2 and 7 above, see also James D. Bratt, ed., *Abraham Kuyper: A Centennial Reader* (Grand Rapids, Mich.: Eerdmans, 1998), 1–16, 205–360, 461–490; Abraham Kuyper, *The Problem of Poverty*, ed. James W. Skillen (Grand Rapids, Mich.: Baker Book House, 1991); and James W. Skillen and Rockne M. McCarthy, eds., *Political Order and the Plural Structure of Society* (Atlanta: Scholar's Press, 1991).

9. To cite only a few of many volumes: Alasdair MacIntyre, *After Virtue: A Study in Moral Theory* (Notre Dame, Ind.: University of Notre Dame Press, 1981); Richard John Neuhaus, *The Naked Public Square: Religion and Democracy in America* (Grand Rapids, Mich.: Eerdmans, 1984); Glenn Tinder, *The Political Meaning of Christianity: An Interpretation* (Baton Rouge: Louisiana State University Press, 1989); Ralph C. Hancock, *Calvin and the Foundations of Modern Politics* (Ithaca, N.Y.: Cornell University Press, 1989); Oliver O'Donovan, *The Desire of the Nations: Rediscovering the Roots of Political Theology* (Cambridge: Cambridge University Press, 1996); Michael J. Sandel, *Democracy's Discontent: America in Search of a Public Philosophy* (Cambridge, Mass.: Harvard University Belknap Press, 1996); Ronald F. Thiemann, *Religion in Public Life: A Dilemma for Democracy* (Washington, D.C.: Georgetown University Press, 1996); Peter L. Berger, ed., *The Desecularization of the World: Resurgent Religion and World Politics* (Grand Rapids, Mich.: Eerdmans, 1999); J. Judd Owen, *Religion and the Demise of Liberal Rationalism* (Chicago: University of Chicago Press, 2001); Robert P. George, *The Clash of Orthodoxies: Law, Religion, and Morality in Crisis* (Wilmington, Del.: ISI Books, 2001); Kraynak, *Christian Faith and Modern Democracy*; David T. Koyzis, *Political Visions and Illusions: A Survey and Critique of Contemporary Ideologies* (Downers Grove, Ill.: InterVarsity Press, 2003); Thomas L. Pangle, *Political Philosophy and the God of Abraham* (Baltimore: Johns Hopkins University Press, 2003).

10. From "The Participation of Catholics in Political Life," a doctrinal note, 24 November 2002, issued by the Congregation for the Doctrine of the Faith, the Vatican.

11. See Paul Marshall, *God and the Constitution: Christianity and American Politics* (Lanham, Md.: Rowman and Littlefield, 2002), 65–89.

12. According to Vatican doctrine, the duty of a Catholic believer is to be "morally coherent" and indivisible in conscience. "There cannot be two parallel lives in [the believer's] existence: on the one hand, the so-called 'spiritual life', with its values and demands; and on the other, the so-called 'secular' life, that is, life in a family, at work, in social responsibilities, in the responsibilities of public life and in culture. The branch, engrafted to the vine which is Christ, bears its fruit in every sphere of existence and activity. In fact, every area of the lay faithful's lives, as different as they are, enters into the plan of God, who desires that these very areas be the 'places in time' where the love of Christ is revealed and realized for both the glory of the Father and service of others." "The Participation of Catholics in Political Life."

13. Robert N. Nelson, *Economics as Religion: From Samuelson to Chicago and Beyond* (University Park, Pa.: Penn State University Press, 2001), 268.

Chapter 2

1. E. J. Dionne Jr., ed., *Community Works: The Revival of Civil Society in America* (Washington, D.C.: Brookings Institution, 1998). A complementary book, containing essays by many of the same authors featured in Dionne's book, is *The Essential Civil Society Reader*, ed. Don E. Eberly (Lanham, Md.: Rowman and Littlefield, 2000).

2. Brian O'Connell, *Civil Society: The Underpinnings of American Democracy* (Hanover, N.H.: University Press of New England, 1999).

3. One of my aims is to address Gertrude Himmelfarb's concern about the expectation that "civil society" can somehow become the answer or "salvation" to all contemporary problems caused by state and market. "I am also wary," she says, "of civil society used as a rhetorical panacea, as if the mere invocation of the term is a solution to all problems—an easy, painless solution, a happy compromise between two extremes." Himmelfarb, "Second Thoughts on Civil Society," in Dionne, *Community Works*, 117.

4. Mary Ann Glendon, *Rights Talk: The Impoverishment of Political Discourse* (New York: Free Press, 1991).

5. Peter L. Berger and Richard John Neuhaus, *To Empower People: The Role of Mediating Structures in Public Policy* (Washington, D.C.: American Enterprise Institute, 1977).

6. Peter F. Drucker, "The Age of Social Transformation," *Atlantic Monthly* (November 1994): 53–80.

7. Dionne, quoting Barber, in *Community Works*, 3.

8. Most recently, the Council on Civil Society, *A Call to Civil Society* (New York: Institute for American Values, 1998), 7.

9. Alan Wolfe, "Is Civil Society Obsolete?" in Dionne, *Community Works*, 17.

10. Alan Wolfe, *Whose Keepers? Social Science and Moral Obligation* (Berkeley: University of California Press, 1989).

11. This report on globalization appeared in *Notes et Documents* (the journal of the International Jacques Maritain Institute) 24, nos. 54–55 (January–August 1999): 42–55.

12. Robert Putnam, *Bowling Alone: The Collapse and Revival of American Community* (New York: Simon and Schuster, 2000).

13. Putnam seems not to see why the very idea of a civic community of tolerant individuals may be the cause of damage to certain kinds of nongovernmental associations that build the strong bonding type of social capital.

Alan Wolfe, like Putnam, also seems less concerned by the evident decline of bonding social capital, believing that "the capacity of Americans to reinvent their worlds" will fill the gaps. "Less likely to find civil society in neighborhoods, families, and churches," says Wolfe, "Americans are more likely to find it at the workplace, in cyberspace, and in forms of political participation that are less organized and more sporadic than traditional political parties." The question that Wolfe agrees cannot be answered now, however, is whether "these newly emerging forms of civil society" can serve as a sufficient "buffer between the market and the state, protecting Americans from the consequences of selfishness on the one hand and coercive altruism on the other." Wolfe, "Is Civil Society Obsolete?" in Dionne, *Community Works*, 22.

14. This is part of the point of Adam Seligman's argument in *The Idea of Civil Society* (Princeton, N.J.: Princeton University Press, 1992). Civil society, he says, is not so easily (if at all) built on the foundation of the ideal of individual autonomy.

15. Amartya Sen, *Development as Freedom* (New York: Anchor Books, 1999).

16. Drucker, "The Age of Social Transformation."

17. Jean Bethke Elshtain, "The Family and Civic Life," in her *Power Trips and Other Journeys: Essays in Feminism as Civic Discourse* (Madison: University of Wisconsin, Press, 1990), 49–56.

18. Michael Sandel, *Liberalism and the Limits of Justice* (Cambridge: Cambridge University Press, 1982). For the wider debate, see Michael Sandel, ed., *Liberalism and Its Critics* (New York: New York University Press, 1984).

19. Elshtain, *Power Trips*, 57.

20. Elshtain, "Not a Cure-All," in Dionne, *Community Works*, 27. For a complementary argument, see Elizabeth Fox-Genovese et al., *Women and the Future of the Family* (Grand Rapids, Mich.: Baker Books, 2000).

21. Elshtain, "Not a Cure-All," 27.

22. Elshtain, "Not a Cure-All," 28.

23. Elshtain, "Not a Cure-All," 29.

24. Alan Whaites, "Heavens Not Havens: Civil Society and Social Change," in *Local Ownership, Global Change: Will Civil Society Save the World?* eds. Roland Hoksbergen and Lowell M. Ewert (Monrovia, Calif.: World Vision, 2002), 143.

25. Himmelfarb, "Second Thoughts," in Dionne, *Community Works*, 119.

26. Thus, Himmelfarb's point that "when we speak of the breakdown of the family, it is a moral breakdown we are talking about. And when we speak of the restoration of civil society, it is a moral restoration we should seek. That restoration may actually take us outside the realm of civil society, for the mediating structures of civil society are themselves dependent on the well-being of the individuals who participate in them and of the state that protects and legitimizes them." "Second Thoughts," in Dionne, *Community Works*, 120.

27. Walzer, "The Idea of Civil Society," in Dionne, *Community Works*, 138, 140. As Himmelfarb puts it, "For good or bad, the state is as much the repository and transmitter of values as are the institutions of civil society. Legislation, judicial decisions, administrative regulations, educational requirements, the tax codes are all instruments of legitimization—or illegitimization." "Second Thoughts," in Dionne, *Community Works*, 121.

For more on the idea of the state in relation to a differentiated society from a Christian-democratic point of view, see Jonathan Chaplin, "Subsidiarity and Sphere Sovereignty: Catholic and Reformed Conceptions of the Role of the State," in *Things Old and New: Catholic Social Teaching*, eds. Francis P. McHugh and Samuel M. Natale (Lanham, Md.: University Press of America, 1997), 175–202; Jonathan Chaplin, "Religion and Democracy," in *Contemporary Political Studies 1998, vol. 2*, eds. Andrew Dobson and Jeffrey Stanyer (Political Studies Association of the United Kingdom, 1998), 988–1003; and Jonathan Chaplin, "Beyond Liberal Restraint: Defending Religiously Based Arguments in Law and Public Policy," *University of British Columbia Law Review* 33, no. 2 (2000).

28. For more on economic development, see Bob Goudzwaard et al., *Globalization and the Kingdom of God* (Grand Rapids: Baker Books, 2001); Bob Goudzwaard and Harry de Lange, *Beyond Poverty and Affluence: Toward an Economy of Care* (Grand Rapids, Mich.: Eerdmans, 1995); and John C. Miller, ed., *Curing World Poverty: The New Role of Property* (St. Louis: Social Justice Review, 1994).

29. Sen, *Development as Freedom*, 279.

30. Himmelfarb, "Second Thoughts," in Dionne, *Community Works*, 118.

31. Whaites, "Heavens Not Havens," in Hoksbergen and Ewert, *Local Ownership*, 150.

Chapter 3

1. See, for example, Eric Voegelin, *The New Science of Politics* (Chicago: University of Chicago Press, 1952); and Voegelin, *From Enlightenment to Revolution*, ed. John H. Hallowell (Durham, N.C.: Duke University Press, 1975).

2. Others who are critics of the idea of human progress or who question the belief that the modern expansion of knowledge has created or coincided with an advance in the quality of human experience include Leszek Kolakowski, *Modernity on Endless Trial* (Chicago: University of Chicago Press, 1990); Harold J. Berman, *Law*

and Revolution: The Formation of the Western Legal Tradition (Cambridge, Mass.: Harvard University Press, 1983); Michael Polanyi, Personal Knowledge: Towards a Post-Critical Philosophy (Chicago: University of Chicago Press, 1958), esp. 327–380; David Novak, Jewish Social Ethics (New York: Oxford University Press, 1992); Vigen Guroian, Ethics After Christendom: Toward an Ecclesial Christian Ethic (Grand Rapids, Mich.: Eerdmans, 1994), esp. 11–52; Robert E. Lane, "The Road Not Taken: Friendship, Consumerism, and Happiness," in Ethics of Compassion: The Good Life, Justice, and Global Stewardship, eds. David A. Crocker and Toby Linden (Lanham, Md.: Rowman and Littlefield, 1998), 226–235; George Parkin Grant, Technology and Justice (Notre Dame, Ind.: University of Notre Dame Press, 1986); Christopher Lasch, The True and Only Heaven: Progress and Its Critics (New York: W. W. Norton, 1991); Robert Nisbet, The Present Age: Progress and Anarchy in Modern America (New York: Harper and Row, 1988).

3. See Stanley W. Carlson-Thies and James W. Skillen, eds., Welfare in America: Christian Perspectives on a Policy in Crisis (Grand Rapids, Mich.: Eerdmans, 1996). For historical coverage of the development of certain American social policies, see Charles L. Glenn, The Myth of the Common School (Amherst: University of Massachusetts Press, 1988); Margaret Weir, Ann Shola Orloff, and Theda Skocpol, The Politics of Social Policy in the United States (Princeton, N.J.: Princeton University Press, 1988); and Paul Starr, The Social Transformation of American Medicine (New York: Basic Books, 1982).

4. The contrasting equality-oriented and freedom-oriented approaches are exemplified on the one side by Theodore R. Marmor, Jerry L. Mashaw, and Philip L. Harvey, America's Misunderstood Welfare State (New York: Basic Books, 1990), and on the other side by Marvin Olasky, The Tragedy of American Compassion (Wheaton, Ill.: Crossway Books, 1992).

5. This is the question that Michael Walzer explores very fruitfully in his Spheres of Justice: A Defense of Pluralism and Equality (New York: Basic Books, 1983).

6. Compare Mary Ann Glendon, Rights Talk: The Impoverishment of Political Discourse (New York: Free Press, 1991); William A. Galston, Liberal Pluralism: The Implications of Value Pluralism for Political Theory and Practice (Cambridge: Cambridge University Press, 2002), and Galston, Liberal Purposes: Goods, Virtues, and Diversity in the Liberal State (New York: Cambridge University Press, 1991); Amitai Etzioni, ed., New Communitarian Thinking: Persons, Virtues, Institutions, and Communities (Charlottesville: University of Virginia Press, 1995); and Elizabeth Frazer and Nicola Lacey, The Politics of Community: A Feminist Critique of the Liberal-Communitarian Debate (Toronto: University of Toronto Press, 1993).

7. The debate over the book by Richard J. Hernstein and Charles Murray, The Bell Curve (New York: Free Press, 1994) is instructive here. The authors and many of their critics assume that human beings are individual behavioral mechanisms to be measured and assessed in terms of various biologically and environmentally abstracted determinants. Hernstein and Murray try to make the case that an unrealistic ideal of social equality has misled policymakers to ignore the fact of certain

genetic and racial differences among people. In the present knowledge society, individuals with higher IQs are getting better jobs and generally doing better economically, and little can be done to change that by social engineering aimed at overcoming racial and other group differences. The "only answer to the problem of group differences," the authors write in a later article, "is an energetic and uncompromising recommitment to individualism." Murray and Hernstein, "Race, Genes and I.Q.—An Apologia," *New Republic*, 31 October 1994, 35.

Some of *The Bell Curve*'s critics think Hernstein and Murray are subtly (or not so subtly) encouraging citizens and governments to give up the fight to overcome racism and economic inequality. In other words, they read the book as a social Darwinist apologia for letting individuals rise or fall, live or die, on their own merits and initiatives. The critics of Hernstein and Murray want more significant government intervention.

Some of the debate over *The Bell Curve* can be found in the critical responses published in the *New Republic*, 31 October 1994. See also Alan Ryan, "Apocalypse Now?" *New York Review of Books*, 17 November 1994, 7–11; Charles Lane, "The Tainted Sources of *The Bell Curve*," *New York Review of Books*, 1 December 1994, 14–19; and "How Clever Is Charles Murray?" *Economist*, 22 October 1994.

8. Marian Wright Edelman, *Families in Peril: An Agenda for Social Change* (Cambridge, Mass.: Harvard University Press, 1987), 33.

9. For a valuable update on the importance of the family for children, particularly the two-parent family, see David P. Gushee, "Rebuilding Marriage and the Family," in *Toward a Just and Caring Society*, ed. David P. Gushee (Grand Rapids, Mich.: Baker Books, 1999), 499–530; Barbara Dafoe Whitehead, "Dan Quayle Was Right," *Atlantic Monthly* (April 1993): 47–84; and David Blankenhorn, Steven Bayme, and Jean Bethke Elshtain, eds., *Rebuilding the Nest: A New Commitment to the American Family* (Milwaukee: Family Service America, 1990).

10. Stressing the importance of a strong family for children must not be played off against women's rights as if the two are incompatible. See Anne Carr and Mary Stewart Van Leeuwen, eds., *Religion, Feminism, and the Family* (Louisville, Ky.: Westminster John Knox Press, 1996); Mary Stewart Van Leeuwen, ed., *After Eden: Facing the Challenge of Gender Reconciliation* (Grand Rapids, Mich.: Eerdmans, 1993), esp. 416–451; Elizabeth Fox-Genovese et al., *Women and the Future of the Family* (Grand Rapids: Baker Books, 2000), and Fox-Genovese, *Feminism Without Illusions: A Critique of Individualism* (Chapel Hill: University of North Carolina Press, 1991); Jean Bethke Elshtain, *Power Trips and Other Journeys: Essays in Feminism as Civic Discourse* (Madison: University of Wisconsin Press, 1990).

11. On the rights of the family, see David Wagner, "The Family and the Constitution" *First Things* (August–September 1994): 23–28; Bruce C. Hafen, "Individualism in Family Law," in *Rebuilding the Nest*, 161–178; Elshtain, "The Family and Civic Life," in *Power Trips*, 45–60. For more on social as well as individual rights see also Mary Ann Glendon, "What's Wrong with Welfare Rights?" and Paul Marshall, "Rights Talk and Welfare Policy," in Carlson-Thies and Skillen, *Welfare in America*,

81–94 and 277–297, respectively; and Paul Marshall, "Two Types of Rights," *Canadian Journal of Political Science* 25, no. 4 (1992): 661–676.

12. Confirming this point through an analysis of unhealthy patterns of development is Cynthia Jones Neal, "Family Issues in Welfare Reform: Developmental Pathways as a Theoretical Framework for Understanding Generational Cycles of Poverty," in Carlson-Thies and Skillen, *Welfare in America*, 318–347.

13. Compare Elshtain, "The Family Crisis and State Intervention: The Construction of Child Abuse as Social Problem and Popular Rhetoric," in *Power Trips*, 73–88, and Mary-Lou Weisman, "When Parents Are Not in the Best Interests of the Child," *Atlantic Monthly* (July 1994), 43–63.

14. See John E. Coons, "The Religious Rights of Children," in *Religious Human Rights in Global Perspective: Religious Perspectives*, eds. John Witte Jr. and Johan van der Vyver (The Hague: Martinus Nijhoff Publishers, 1996), 157–174.

15. On parental rights in education, see Charles L. Glenn, "Free Schools and the Revival of Urban Communities," in Carlson-Thies and Skillen, *Welfare in America*, 393–425; John E. Coons and Stephen Sugarman, *Education by Choice: The Case for Family Control* (Berkeley: University of California Press, 1978); James W. Skillen, ed., *The School-Choice Controversy: What Is Constitutional?* (Grand Rapids, Mich.: Baker Books, 1993); and Barbara Dafoe Whitehead, "The Failure of Sex Education," *Atlantic Monthly* (October 1994), 55–80.

16. "A New Vision for Welfare Reform," in Carlson-Thies and Skillen, *Welfare in America*, 565–569.

17. On the question of an emerging (or hardening) "culture of poverty" in the United States as it relates to the failure of individuals and various nongovernment institutions to fulfill their responsibilities, see Lawrence M. Mead, *Beyond Entitlement: The Social Obligations of Citizenship* (New York: Free Press, 1986); Cynthia Jones Neal, "Family Issues in Welfare Reform," in Carlson-Thies and Skillen, *Welfare in America*, 318–347; Daniel Patrick Moynihan, *Family and Nation* (New York: Harcourt Brace Jovanovich, 1986); David T. Ellwood, *Poor Support: Poverty in the American Family* (New York: Basic Books, 1988), esp. 189–230.

Chapter 4

1. The Center for Public Justice has published at least twenty different books, booklets, and guides related to welfare reform and Charitable Choice, including *Charitable Choice for Welfare and Community Services: An Implementation Guide for State, Local, and Federal Officials* (2001). See the Center's website at www.cpjustice.org. See also, most recently, Dave Donaldson and Stanley Carlson-Thies, *A Revolution of Compassion: Faith-Based Groups as Full Partners in Fighting America's Social Problems* (Grand Rapids, Mich.: Baker Books, 2003).

2. Two books in particular help to highlight the controversy through the voices of those in contention. See Stephen V. Monsma and J. Christopher Soper, eds., *Equal*

Treatment of Religion in a Pluralistic Society (Grand Rapids, Mich.: Eerdmans, 1998), and Derek Davis and Barry Hankins, eds., *Welfare Reform and Faith-Based Organizations* (Waco, Tex.: J. M. Dawson Institute of Church-State Studies, Baylor University, 1999).

3. For a detailed study, see John Witte Jr., *Religion and the American Constitutional Experiment: Essential Rights and Liberties* (Boulder, Colo.: Westview Press, 2000), 7–100. See also Donald S. Lutz, *The Origins of American Constitutionalism* (Baton Rouge: Louisiana State University Press, 1988).

4. For more on this matter of state disestablishment, see Witte, *Religion*, 93–96.

5. See Rockne M. McCarthy, James W. Skillen, and William A. Harper, *Disestablishment a Second Time: Genuine Pluralism for American Schools* (Grand Rapids, Mich.: Eerdmans, 1982), 15–52.

6. Ibid., 52–72. See Diane Ravitch, *The Great School Wars: New York City, 1805–1973* (New York: Basic Books, 1974), 3–91, and Charles L. Glenn, *The Myth of the Common School* (Amherst: University of Massachusetts Press, 1988).

7. Parental primacy or "principalship" in education as well as governmental primacy in education are both upheld in the law, quite incompatibly. See McCarthy, Skillen, and Harper, *Disestablishment*, 103–106, 124–136; Stephen Arons, *Compelling Belief: The Culture of American Schooling* (Amherst: University of Massachusetts Press, 1986); and "Conference Proceedings: *Pierce*, Pluralism, and Partnership," from a conference to commemorate the seventy-fifth anniversary of the *Pierce* decision (Washington, D.C.: U.S. Department of Education, 2001). The 1925 *Pierce* decision was *Pierce v. Society of the Sisters of the Holy Names of Jesus and Mary*, 268 U.S. 510 (1925).

8. See especially Stanley W. Carlson-Thies, "Charitable Choice: Bringing Religion Back into American Welfare," *Journal of Policy History* 13, no. 1 (2001), 109–132.

9. Ellen Willis, "Freedom from Religion: What's at Stake in Faith-Based Politics," *The Nation*, 19 February 2001.

10. On the non-neutrality of every point of view, see Rockne M. McCarthy et al., *Society, State, and Schools: A Case for Structural and Confessional Pluralism* (Grand Rapids, Mich.: Eerdmans, 1981), 107–120, and Roy A. Clouser, *The Myth of Religious Neutrality* (Notre Dame, Ind.: University of Notre Dame Press, 1991).

11. See Stephen V. Monsma, *Positive Neutrality* (Westport, Conn.: Greenwood Press, 1993).

12. As Kate O'Beirne says, "Catholic Charities—one of the nation's largest social-welfare groups—contracts with government welfare agencies to deliver social services, and is scrupulously secular in dealing with its needy clients. The Salvation Army puts up a wall of separation between its social outreach—which includes a spiritual dimension—and its publicly funded programs, where Bible reading and prayer meetings are strictly forbidden." "Church (Groups) and State: The Problem with the Faith-Based Bit," *National Review*, 19 February 2001. See also John A. Coleman, "American Catholicism, Catholic Charities U.S.A., and Welfare Reform," *Journal of Policy History* 13, no. 1 (2001), 73–108.

13. Ashley Woodiwiss, "Democracy Agonistes," *Books and Culture* (March/April 2001), 24. Nicholas Wolterstorff critiques this kind of liberal thinking in his discussion with Robert Audi in their book, *Religion in the Public Square: The Place of Religious Convictions in Political Debate* (Lanham, Md.: Rowman and Littlefield, 1997). See the fine review of this and several related books by Brian Stiltner, "Reassessing Religion's Place in a Liberal Democracy," *Religious Studies Review* (October 2000): 319–325.

14. Peter Dobkin Hall, "Diminished Authority: Church, State, and Accountability," *Nonprofit Times* (March 2001): 45.

15. For some of the background of what follows see James W. Skillen and Rockne M. McCarthy, eds., *Political Order and the Plural Structure of Society* (Atlanta: Scholars Press, 1991); Stanley W. Carlson-Thies and James W. Skillen, eds., *Welfare in America: Christian Perspectives on a Policy in Crisis* (Grand Rapids, Mich.: Eerdmans, 1996); and Charles L. Glenn, *The Ambiguous Embrace: Government and Faith-Based Schools and Social Agencies* (Princeton, N.J.: Princeton University Press, 2000).

16. I certainly agree with Hall ("Diminished Authority") that faith-based organizations should not be granted relief from health, safety, and fiduciary requirements that would apply to groups that make no religious claims for their work. But the opposite should also be true, namely, that government-owned and "secular" nonprofits should not be granted privileges denied to faith-based organizations because the latter are "religious." The question is how to remove religious (or viewpoint) discrimination while also doing justice to the integrity of every nongovernment organization and to all citizens. For more on this, see Glenn, *Ambiguous Embrace*, 99–130 and 266–296.

17. Quoted in the *Washington Post*, 12 March 2001.

18. From the executive summary of "Corrupting Charity," Briefing Paper No. 62, by Michael Tanner, Cato Institute, Washington, D.C., 22 March 2001.

19. See Carl H. Esbeck, "Religion and the First Amendment: Some Causes of the Recent Confusion," *William and Mary Law Review* 42, no. 3 (March 2001): 907–914, and Esbeck, "The Establishment Clause as a Structural Restraint on Governmental Power," *Iowa Law Review* 84, no. 1 (October 1998): 1–113. For more on the First Amendment and whether there is one clause or two, see Esbeck, "Differentiating the Free Exercise and Establishment Clauses," *Journal of Church and State* 42 (Spring 2000): 311–334; Stephen V. Monsma, "Substantive Neutrality as a Basis for Free Exercise-No Establishment Common Ground," *Journal of Church and State* 42 (Winter 2000): 13–35.

20. See Richard A. Baer Jr., "The Supreme Court's Discriminatory Use of the Term 'Sectarian,'" *Journal of Law and Politics* 6, no. 3 (Spring 1990): 449–468.

Chapter 5

1. Quoted in James T. Patterson, *Brown v. Board of Education: A Civil Rights Milestone and Its Troubled Legacy* (New York: Oxford University Press, 2001), xiv.

2. When Eldridge Cleaver was about to return to the United States after years in exile, he explained his motive: "Those of us who developed a psychology of opposition must take a pause and sum up our experiences. We must recognize that in a sense we are playing in a brand new ball game. The slogans of yesterday will not get us through the tasks at hand" (*New York Times*, 18 November 1975). This is, of course, at the heart of the problem in the struggle over affirmative action. See Drew S. Days III, "Affirmative Action," in *Civil Liberties in Conflict*, ed. Larry Gostin (New York: Routledge, 1988), 85–101; Glenn C. Loury, "Affirmative Action: Is It Just? Does It Work?" in *The Constitutional Bases of Political and Social Change in the United States*, ed. Shlomo Slonimn (New York: Praeger, 1990), 109–139; Stephen L. Carter, *Reflections of an Affirmative Action Baby* (New York: Basic Books, 1991); and Shelby Steele, *The Content of Our Character* (New York: St. Martin's Press, 1990). A good collection of views on all sides of the affirmative action debate can be found in George E. Curry, ed., *The Affirmative Action Debate* (Reading, Mass.: Addison-Wesley, 1996).

3. Compare, for example, the different emphases of the following authors: Glenn C. Loury, *One by One, From the Inside Out: Essays and Reviews on Race and Responsibility in America* (New York: Free Press, 1995); Nicholas Lemann, *The Promised Land: The Great Black Migration and How It Changed America* (New York: Knopf, 1991); Jim Sleeper, *The Closest of Strangers: Liberalism and the Politics of Race in New York* (New York: W. W. Norton, 1990); Andrew Hacker, *Two Nations: Black and White, Separate, Hostile, Unequal* (New York: Scribners, 1992); and Steele, *Content of Our Character*.

4. Kiini Ibura Salaam, "Race, a Discussion in Ten Parts, Plus a Few Moments of Unsubstantiated Theory and One Inarguable Fact," in *When Race Becomes Real: Black and White Writers Confront Their Personal Histories*, ed. Bernestine Singley (Chicago: Lawrence Hill Books, 2002), 259–260.

5. Kimberly Springer, "Talking White," in Singley, *When Race Becomes Real*, 78.

6. David Brion Davis, *In the Image of God: Religion, Moral Values, and Our Heritage of Slavery* (New Haven, Conn.: Yale University Press, 2001), 63–64.

7. Davis, *Image of God*, 63.

8. Frederick Douglass, *Narrative of the Life of Frederick Douglass, an American Slave* (New York: Barnes and Noble, 2002, 1845), 121.

9. Davis, *Image of God*, 63. For a detailed discussion of differences between northern and southern Christians over slavery, see Mark A. Noll, *America's God: From Jonathan Edwards to Abraham Lincoln* (New York: Oxford University Press, 2002), 367–438, and Eugene D. Genovese, *A Consuming Fire: The Fall of the Confederacy in the Mind of the White Christian South* (Athens: University of Georgia Press, 1999).

10. One can make distinctions between the relative significance of the court decisions compared to congressional legislation, as has Gerard N. Rosenberg in *The Hollow Hope* (Chicago: University of Chicago Press, 1991). He concludes that court decisions such as the U.S. Supreme Court's *Brown v. Board of Education* had virtually no direct effect on segregation before Congress took action. This is not to underestimate the significance of executive action, such as Eisenhower's calling out the National Guard in Little Rock.

11. See, for example, Joseph C. Hough Jr., *Black Power and White Protestants* (New York: Oxford University Press, 1968), which shows the very limited ability of white Protestants to respond to the Black Power movement. In this respect, it is worth considering Charles A. Lofgren's argument in *The Plessy Case: A Legal-Historical Interpretation* (New York: Oxford University Press, 1987) that the Supreme Court's 1890s "separate but equal" ruling nonetheless contained seeds of the civil rights transformation of the twentieth century.

12. See Stephen B. Oates, *Let the Trumpet Sound: The Life of Martin Luther King, Jr.* (New York: New American Library, 1982); Andrew Michael Manis, *Southern Civil Religions in Conflict: Black and White Baptists and Civil Rights, 1947–1957* (Athens: University of Georgia Press, 1987); and Jesse L. Jackson, *Straight from the Heart* (Philadelphia: Fortress Press, 1987), passim.

13. Manis, *Southern Civil Religions*, 3.

14. Manis, *Southern Civil Religions*, 13.

15. As the background for what follows, see my *The Scattered Voice: Christians at Odds in the Public Square* (Grand Rapids, Mich.: Zondervan, 1990), esp. chap. 6, "Civil Rights Reformers"; and my *Recharging the American Experiment: Principled Pluralism for Genuine Civic Community* (Grand Rapids, Mich.: Baker Books, 1994), esp. chap. 7, "Individual and Institutional Rights."

16. In addition to Patterson's book on *Brown*, also see Richard Kluger, *Simple Justice* (New York: Vintage Books, 1975).

17. On 1 September 1998, federal district court judge Peter J. Messitte ordered an end to mandatory busing in Prince George's County, Maryland. The ruling met with approval on all sides, reflecting changed circumstances since the 1970s when court-ordered busing went into effect. Janette Bell, an African American and president of the county's education association, commented that "one of the negatives [of busing] was that when kids were moved so far away from home, parents were no longer involved in the schools." *Washington Post*, 2 September 1998.

In the fall of 1998 in Washington, D.C., a growing number of parents were seeking access to new charter schools. One reason, as Angelia Orr explained, is that she "dreaded September, when [her daughter] Ashlee would have to travel six miles through notoriously dangerous streets to Roper Middle School in Northeast." *Washington Times*, 28 August 1998.

18. The diverse range of cultures, communities, towns, school districts, and rural and urban ethnic enclaves across America is astounding, and thus no generalization about the relation between family and school will hold up everywhere. An early opponent of segregation in the South, novelist and critic Walker Percy, offers keen insight into the difference in the social meaning of the school for whites in the North in contrast to whites in the South in his essay "The Southern Moderate," in *Walker Percy: Sign-Posts in a Strange Land*, ed. Patrick Samway (New York: Noonday Press, 1991), 94–101. In the South, Percy wrote in 1957, the school body corresponded far more to the social body than it did in the North. Especially in northern urban areas, the school was a place where people sent their children to receive certain services. In

the South, the school was much less differentiated from the community. This is one reason why the desegregation of schools required different approaches and sensitivities in different parts of the country.

19. For expression of, or assessment of, civil-religious nationalism, see Manis, *Southern Civil Religions*; Jackson, *Straight from the Heart*; Ruth H. Bloch, "Religion and Ideological Change in the American Revolution," in *Religion and American Politics: From the Colonial Period to the 1980s*, ed. Mark A. Noll (New York: Oxford University Press, 1990), 44–61; Sidney E. Mead "The 'Nation with the Soul of a Church,'" and David Little, "The Origins of Perplexity: Civil Religion and Moral Belief in the Thought of Thomas Jefferson," both in *American Civil Religion*, eds. Russell E. Richey and Donald C. Jones (New York: Harper Forum Books, 1974), 45–75 and 185–210; and Walker Percy, "Stoicism in the South," in *Walker Percy*, 83–88.

20. On the idea of the political community as a pluralist unity or community of communities, see Michael Walzer, "A Community of Communities," in *Debating Democracy's Discontent: Essays on American Politics, Law and Public Philosophy*, eds. Anita L. Allen and Milton C. Regan (New York: Oxford University Press, 1998); and James W. Skillen and Rockne M. McCarthy, eds., *Political Order and the Plural Structure of Society* (Atlanta: Scholars Press, 1991), 1–27 and passim.

Chapter 6

1. See Charles Glenn, *The Myth of the Common School* (Amherst: University of Massachusetts Press, 1988).

2. The phrase "rising tide of mediocrity" is from the report of the National Commission on Excellence in Education, *A Nation at Risk: The Imperative for Educational Reform* (Washington, D.C.: U.S. Government Printing Office, 1983).

3. John Chubb and Terry Moe, *Politics, Markets, and America's Schools* (Washington, D.C.: Brookings Institution, 1990). See also Myron Lieberman, *Privatization and Educational Choice* (New York: St. Martin's Press, 1989).

4. See, for example, Robert B. Everhart, ed., *The Public School Monopoly: A Critical Analysis of Education and the State in American Society* (San Francisco: Pacific Institute for Public Policy Research, 1982).

5. See Amy Gutmann, *Democratic Education* (Princeton, N.J.: Princeton University Press, 1989), and Diane Ravitch, *The Great School Wars* (New York: Basic Books, 1974), 251–378.

6. The First Amendment to the U.S. Constitution provides that "Congress shall make no law respecting an establishment of religion, or prohibiting the free exercise thereof."

7. See James B. Conant, *Thomas Jefferson and the Development of American Public Education* (Los Angeles: University of California Press, 1970); Daniel Webster, "On the Education of Youth in America," and Benjamin Rush, "Plan for the Establishment of Public Schools," both in *Essays on Education in the Early Republic*, ed. Frederick Rudolph (Cambridge, Mass.: Harvard University Press, 1965).

8. See Rockne M. McCarthy, James W. Skillen, and William A. Harper, *Disestablishment a Second Time: Genuine Pluralism for American Schools* (Grand Rapids, Mich.: Eerdmans, 1982). See also Glenn, *Myth*, 63–145, and Robert Healey, *Jefferson on Religion in Public Education* (New Haven, Conn.: Yale University Press, 1962).

9. See, for example, Jefferson, "Notes on Virginia," in *The Life and Selected Writings of Thomas Jefferson*, eds. Adrienne Koch and William Peden (New York: Modern Library, 1944), 262–266.

10. Jefferson, "Notes on Virginia," in *Selected Writings*, 274–275.

11. See Jefferson's letters to George Wythe (13 August 1786), Joseph Priestly (27 January 1800), and Peter Carr (7 September 1814), in *Selected Writings*, 394–395, 554–555, and 642–649, respectively.

12. Jefferson, Letter to Thomas Law (13 June 1814), "Notes on Virginia," and Letter to Benjamin Rush (23 September 1800), in *Selected Writings*, 636–638, 265, and 558, respectively.

13. See, for example, Jefferson's letter to William Short (31 October 1819), in *Selected Writings*, 693–697.

14. Jefferson, "Act for Establishing Religious Freedom" (1779), in *Selected Writings*, and Letter to Peter Carr (10 August 1787), in *Selected Writings*, 311–313, 429–433, respectively.

15. Jefferson, Letter to James Madison (20 December 1787); Letter to William Bache (2 February 1800); Letter to Baron Alexander von Humboldt (13 June 1817); Letter to James Smith (8 December 1822), in *Selected Writings*, 440, 556, 681, and 703, respectively.

16. See, Conant, *Thomas Jefferson*, 88–93; Rudolph, *Essays*, ix–xxi; Healey, *Jefferson on Religion and Public Education*, 187; and Robert D. Heslep, *Thomas Jefferson and Education* (New York: Random House, 1969), 88.

17. Jefferson, Letter to John Adams (28 October 1813), in *Selected Writings*, 632–634.

18. Jefferson, Letter to John Adams (28 October 1813), in *Selected Writings*, 634.

19. David B. Tyack, ed., *Turning Points in American Educational History* (Lexington, Mass.: Xerox College Publishing, 1967), 85.

20. See Healey, *Jefferson on Religion and Public Education*, 159–177.

21. Jefferson, Letter to William Short (31 October 1822), in *Selected Writings*, 694.

22. For more on the religion's influence and involvement in education in early America, see Glenn, *Myth*, 146–178.

23. Glenn, *Myth*, 179–204.

24. See generally McCarthy, Skillen, Harper, *Disestablishment*, 53–72, and Ravitch, *The Great School Wars*, 3–76.

25. For more on this case, see Stephen Arons, "The Separation of School and State: *Pierce* Reconsidered," *Harvard Educational Review* 46 (1976), and Arons, *Compelling Belief: The Culture of American Schooling* (Amherst: University of Massachusetts Press, 1986).

26. According to the *Pierce* majority decision, "The child is not the mere creature of the State; those who nurture him and direct his destiny have the right to prepare the child to fill his place in society." *Pierce v. Society of Sisters*, 268 U.S. 510 (1925), 535.

27. However, the Court did not rule that states could not have the primary role in education. To the contrary: "No question is raised concerning the power of the State reasonably to regulate all schools." *Pierce v. Society of Sisters*, 534.

28. See *Mueller v. Allen*, 463 U.S. 388 (1983), holding that states can permit the deduction of expenses for tuition, textbooks, and transportation from state income taxes; *Lemon v. Kurtzman*, 411 U.S. 192 (1973), establishing a three-part test to determine whether government money for services at a religious school violates the establishment clause of the First Amendment; and *Board of Education v. Allen*, 392 U.S. 236 (1968), permitting the loan of public-school textbooks to parents of children attending nonpublic schools.

29. See *Mergens v. Board of Education*, 867 F.2d 1076 (8th Cir.), cert. granted, 109 S. Ct. 3240 (1989), requiring a public school to allow students to use its premises for a Christian Bible study meeting.

30. On the non-neutrality of education, see Richard A. Baer Jr., "American Public Education and the Myth of Value Neutrality," in *Democracy and the Renewal of Public Education*, ed. Richard John Neuhaus (Grand Rapids, Mich.: Eerdmans, 1987).

31. Chubb and Moe, *Politics, Markets*.

32. Jefferson, Letter to James Madison (20 December 1787), Letter to Baron Alexander von Humboldt (13 June 1817), and "Notes on Virginia," in *Selected Writings*, 440–441, 681, and 262–265, respectively.

33. See Rockne M. McCarthy et al., *Society, State, and Schools: A Case for Structural and Confessional Pluralism* (Grand Rapids, Mich.: Eerdmans, 1981).

34. See, for example, *Sims v. Virginia Electric Power Co.*, 550 F.2d 929, 933 (4th Cir.), cert. denied, 431 U.S. 925 (1977), interpreting Virginia law as imposing the duty to support a child on both father and mother; *Alexander v. Alexander*, 494 So. 2d 365 (Miss. 1986), ruling that the duty of parents to support a child is a continuing legal and moral obligation and is a vested right of the child; *In re Estate of Peterson*, 66 Wis. 2d 535, 540, 225 N.W.2d 644, 646 (1975): "Under the common law, parents had and have a legal obligation to support and maintain their minor children under certain circumstances."; Alaska Stat. § 25.20.030 (1983), articulating the duty of a parent to maintain the child; Conn. Gen. Stat. § 45–43 (1981), stating that father and mother are joint natural guardians with duties and obligations; Md. Fam. Law Code Ann. § 5-203 (1984), stating that parents are joint natural guardians.

35. See James Coleman and Thomas Hoffer, *Public and Private High Schools: The Impact of Communities* (New York: Basic Books, 1987), comparing government-run and independent high schools; Glenn, *Myth*, 207–235, discussing early alternatives to the common schools; Michael Katz, *Class, Bureaucracy, and Schools: The Illusion of Educational Change in America* (New York: Praeger, 1975), 3–55, discussing four different types of school structures existing in America prior to the organization of

public systems after the 1840s; and Ravitch, *The Great School Wars*, 3–76, outlining the circumstances of independent schooling in New York City prior to 1842.

36. See, for example, *Whitfield v. Simpson*, 312 F. Supp. 889 (D. Ill. 1970), finding that teachers and school officials bear the same responsibility for children as do parents, in upholding the constitutionality of a statute permitting expulsion from school for gross misconduct. The Supreme Court, however, has overruled several state court determinations that school officials acted *in loco parentis* for purposes of Fourth Amendment immunity. See *New Jersey v. T.L.O.*, 469 U.S. 325 (1985). Justice White, writing for eight members of the Court, said, "More generally, the Court has recognized that 'the concept of parental delegation' as a source of school authority is not entirely 'consonant with compulsory education laws'" (336). Today's public school officials do not merely exercise authority voluntarily conferred on them by individual parents; rather they act in furtherance of publicly mandated educational and disciplinary policies.

37. For more discussion of religious freedom, group rights, and establishment clause interpretation, see John Witte Jr., *Religion and the American Constitutional Experiment* (Boulder, Colo.: Westview Press, 2000); Carl Esbeck, "Establishment Clause Limits on Governmental Interference with Religious Organizations," *Washington and Lee Law Review* 41 (1984), 347–420, and Esbeck, "Religion and the Neutral State: Imperative or Impossibility," *Cumberland Law Review* 15 (1984–85).

38. For a more elaborate discussion of present and future alternatives, see Charles L. Glenn, *The Ambiguous Embrace: Government and Faith-Based Schools and Social Agencies* (Princeton, N.J.: Princeton University Press, 2000); John Coons and Stephen Sugarman, *Education by Choice: The Case for Family Control* (Berkeley: University of California Press, 1978); and McCarthy et al., *Society, State, and Schools*, 136–144, 170–208.

Chapter 7

1. Robert D. Kaplan, "The Coming Anarchy," *Atlantic Monthly* (February 1994): 54, 58.

2. Robert H. Nelson interprets the rise of the environmental movement as one of the signs of crisis in modern, progressive economics, which has become the religion of our day: *Economics as Religion: From Samuelson to Chicago and Beyond* (University Park, Pa.: Penn State University Press, 2001), esp. 303–338.

3. For an excellent introduction to, and critique of, liberalism, see David T. Koyzis, *Political Visions and Illusions: A Survey and Christian Critique of Contemporary Ideologies* (Downers Grove, Ill.: InterVarsity Press, 2003), 42–71, 124–151.

4. Quotations here from John Locke's "Second Treatise of Civil Government" are from the Hafner Library of Classics edition: *Two Treatises of Government*, ed. Thomas I. Cook (New York: Hafner Press, 1973).

5. See Janel M. Curry-Roper and Steven McGuire, "The Individualistic Imagination and Natural Resource Policy," *Society and Natural Resources* 6 (1993): 259–272.

6. Leo Strauss, *Natural Right and History* (Chicago: University of Chicago Press, 1953), 240–241.

7. Strauss, *Natural Right*, 245–246. Because the ideology of human progress through ever increasing production and consumption is so strong in the West and much of the rest of the world today, the way in which environmentalists have to make their arguments is by heightening the sense of approaching doom and cataclysm. In other words, the ethic they call for is one of *survival* (and thus the need to save the environment). This is not enough, according to Bob Goudzwaard, who wants to go deeper to find an ethic of responsibility and stewardship, not a mere ethic of survival: Goudzwaard, *Capitalism and Progress: A Diagnosis of Western Society*, trans. and ed. Josina Van Nuis Zylstra (Grand Rapids, Mich.: Eerdmans, 1979), 121–129.

8. See Christopher B. Barrett and John C. Bergstrom, "The Economics of God's Creation," *Bulletin of the Association of Christian Economists*, no. 31 (Spring 1998), 4–23, which includes an extensive bibliography, and Timothy D. Terrell, "The Origin of Property Rights: A Critique of Rothbard and Hoppe on Natural Rights," *Faith and Economics* (a review published by the Association of Christian Economists), no. 36 (Fall 2000), 1–9.

9. Calvin DeWitt, "Caring for Creation," *Prism* (December–January 1993–1994), and DeWitt, *Caring for Creation: Responsible Stewardship of God's Handiwork* (Grand Rapids: Baker Books, 1998), 43–47. See also David Novak, *Jewish Social Ethics* (New York: Oxford University Press, 1992), 143–152, 206–220, and Emil B. Berendt, "Using Genesis to Teach Religious Aspects of Economics," *Faith and Economics*, no. 42 (Fall 2003), 40–46.

10. On the contrast here, see Paul Marshall, *God and the Constitution: Christianity and American Politics* (Lanham, Md.: Rowman and Littlefield, 2002), 21–36, and James Skillen, "Going Beyond Liberalism to Christian Social Philosophy," *Christian Scholar's Review* 19, no. 3 (March 1990): 220–230.

11. Another way to put this is to say, as Michael Sandel does, that there are some things money can't buy. In other words, not everything can be "commodified" and thus the law needs to do more than guard and protect persons and their properties. See Sandel, "What Money Shouldn't Buy," *Hedgehog Review* 5, no. 2 (Summer 2003), 77–97.

12. Nelson, *Economics as Religion*, 326.

Chapter 8

1. W. Lance Bennett, *The Governing Crisis: Media, Money, and Marketing in American Elections* (New York: St. Martin's Press, 1992), 14.

2. George F. Will, *Restoration: Congress, Term Limits and the Recovery of Deliberative Democracy* (New York: Free Press, 1992), 110.

3. Will, *Restoration*, 117.

4. Will, *Restoration*, 117. See also William Greider, *Who Will Tell the People? The Betrayal of American Democracy* (New York: Simon and Schuster, 1992), 35–59.

5. James L. Sundquist, *Constitutional Reform and Effective Government*, rev. ed. (Washington, D.C.: Brookings Institution, 1992), 178–179.

6. Will, *Restoration*, 92.

7. Will, *Restoration*, 92.

8. See E. J. Dionne Jr., *Why Americans Hate Politics* (New York: Simon and Schuster, 1991), 136–137. This criticism is not of recent vintage; see, for example, David Broder, *The Party's Over: The Failure of Politics in America* (New York: Harper and Row, 1971), and Martin P. Wattenberg, *The Decline of American Political Parties, 1952–1984* (Cambridge, Mass.: Harvard University Press, 1986).

9. See Sundquist, *Constitutional Reform*, 177–182, and Bennett, *Governing Crisis*, 185–186.

10. Bennett, *Governing Crisis*, 163. See also Ruy A. Teixeira, *The Disappearing American Voter* (Washington, D.C.: Brookings Institution, 1992), 1–57, and Walter Dean Burnham, "The Turnout Problem," in *Elections American Style*, ed. A. James Reichley (Washington, D.C.: Brookings Institution, 1987), 97–133.

11. Bennett, *Governing Crisis*, 163. See also Martin P. Wattenberg, *The Rise of Candidate-Centered Politics* (Cambridge, Mass.: Harvard University Press, 1991).

12. Will, *Restoration*, 19. Will's criticism here is related to the problems associated with campaign financing and media manipulation that Bennett criticizes in detail, *Governing Crisis*, 40–66. See Larry Sabato, "Real and Imagined Corruption in Campaign Financing," in *Elections American Style*, 155–179.

13. Bennett, *Governing Crisis*, 5–6.

14. Bennett, *Governing Crisis*, 9. According to Bennett, "Instead of a principled national leadership with the power to govern by keeping the factions at bay, the leadership has been captured by the factions themselves. Therefore, instead of leading and governing, elected officials cannot do much beyond getting themselves reelected, and in order to do that, they must fashion the most delicate kind of political promises: the kind they cannot possibly hope to keep" (64).

15. Bennett, *Governing Crisis*, 175. For a detailed argument explaining this form of declining government, see Theodore J. Lowi, *The End of Liberalism: The Second Republic of the United States* (New York: W. W. Norton, 1979).

16. For an introduction to proportional representation (PR) as it might affect American politics, see Michael Lind, "A Radical Plan to Change American Politics," *Atlantic Monthly* (August 1992): 73–83; Douglas Amy, *Real Choices/New Voices: The Case for Proportional Representation Elections in the United States* (New York: Columbia University Press, 1993); and Steven Hill, *Fixing Elections: The Failure of America's Winner Take All Politics* (New York: Routledge, 2002). See also Joseph F. Zimmerman, "The Federal Voting Rights Act and Alternative Election Systems," *William and Mary Law Review* 19, no. 4 (Summer 1978): 621–660. For more detailed historical and comparative background, see Douglas Amy, *Behind the Ballot Box: A Citizen's Guide to Voting Systems* (Westport, Conn.: Praeger, 2000); Kathleen Barber, *A Right to Representation: Proportional Election Systems for the Twenty-First Century* (Columbus: Ohio State University Press, 2000); and Arend

Lijphart and Bernard Grofman, eds., *Choosing an Electoral System: Issues and Alternatives* (New York: Praeger, 1984).

17. Changing from the American electoral system of single-member districts to a system of proportional representation for elections to the House of Representatives should not be confounded with the idea of changing from a presidential to a parliamentary system of government. The two do not have to go hand in hand. See Lind, "Radical Plan," and Bennett, *Governing Crisis*, 204–205, both of whom support a change to PR for elections to the House, though Bennett does not develop a plan and Lind adds other details of complexity to the idea that seem to me unnecessary.

18. The change to PR for federal elections to the House of Representatives is even less complicated than implementing term limits. No constitutional amendment is necessary for a change to PR. See the U.S. Constitution, Art. I, Sec. 4; Lind, "Radical Plan," 76.

19. The impossibility of achieving minority representation in a majority-rule electoral system is explained by John R. Low-Beer, "The Constitutional Imperative of Proportional Representation," *Yale Law Journal* 94, no. 1 (November 1984): 172–182. In the United States, the concern about minority representation relates primarily to attempts to gerrymander single-member voting districts, often at court order, in order to achieve some kind of racial representation in a state. In addition to Low-Beer's fine article, see Sanford Levinson, "Gerrymandering and the Brooding Omnipresence of Proportional Representation: Why Won't It Go Away?" *UCLA Law Review* 33 (1985): 257–281; David R. Eichenthal, "Equal Protection III: Voting Rights, Political Gerrymandering, and Proportional Representation," *Annual Survey of American Law* (1987), 93–116; Zimmerman, "Federal Voting Rights Act," 626–640; and Lani Guinier, *Lift Every Voice: Turning a Civil Rights Setback into a New Vision of Social Justice* (New York: Simon and Schuster, 1998).

20. For background here, see Bennett, *Governing Crisis*, 50–64.

21. See Richard S. Katz, "The Single Transferable Vote and Proportional Representation," in Lijphart and Grofman, *Choosing an Electoral System*, 137.

22. On the subject of thresholds, see Arend Lijphart and R. W. Gibberd, "Thresholds and Payoffs in List Systems of Proportional Representation," *European Journal of Political Research* 5 (1977): 219–244.

23. On this point, see Enid Lakeman, "The Case for Proportional Representation," in Lijphart and Grofman, *Choosing an Electoral System*, 46–47.

24. This is related to George Will's complaint about gerrymandering, but Will does not seem to realize that term limits will not even touch the problems associated with gerrymandering. See Will, *Restoration*, 40–50.

25. On the German system, see Eckhard Jesse, "The West German Electoral System: The Case for Reform, 1949–87," *West European Politics* 10 (1987): 434–448; and Max Kaase, "Personalized Proportional Representation: The 'Model' of the West German Electoral System," in Lijphart and Grofman, *Choosing an Electoral System*, 155–164.

26. For the purpose of simplicity in my proposal, I am also foregoing consideration of another very responsible reform, which is to augment representation by enlarging the House beyond its current limit of 435 seats. Michael Lind, for example, points out that if the United States today had the same proportion of population for each representative in the House as it did at the country's founding, there would now be eight thousand seats in the House. "Radical Plan," 75–77. That is far too many, of course, but given the proportions in other countries, there is no reason why we should not have five hundred or seven hundred or even one thousand members in the House. Given the current crisis of confidence in government, however, the first reaction of many citizens to this idea would probably be fear—the fear that a larger number of House members would only add to the gridlock, corruption, and budget-busting tendencies of Congress. There is little point in considering such a change before evidence can be accumulated to show that strong national parties are able to exercise sufficient discipline and responsibility to make possible the enlargement of the House. Once it can be established that PR has helped restore government accountability, then a greater number of House seats would mean better rather than worse representation of the people.

Bibliography

Amy, Douglas. *Behind the Ballot Box: A Citizen's Guide to Voting Systems*. Westport, Conn.: Praeger, 2000.

———. *Real Choices/New Voices: The Case for Proportional Representation Elections in the United States*. New York: Columbia University Press, 1993.

Arons, Stephen. *Compelling Belief: The Culture of American Schooling*. Amherst: University of Massachusetts Press, 1986.

———. "The Separation of School and State: *Pierce* Reconsidered." *Harvard Educational Review* 46 (1976).

Baer, Richard A., Jr. "The Supreme Court's Discriminatory Use of the Term 'Sectarian.'" *Journal of Law and Politics* 6, no. 3 (Spring 1990): 449–468.

Barber, Kathleen. *A Right to Representation: Proportional Election Systems for the Twenty-First Century*. Columbus: Ohio State University Press, 2000.

Bennett, W. Lance. *The Governing Crisis: Media, Money, and Marketing in American Elections*. New York: St. Martin's Press, 1992.

Berger, Peter L., ed. *The Desecularization of the World: Resurgent Religion and World Politics*. Grand Rapids, Mich.: Eerdmans, 1999.

Berger, Peter L., and Richard John Neuhaus. *To Empower People: The Role of Mediating Structures in Public Policy*. Washington, D.C.: American Enterprise Institute, 1977.

Berman, Harold J. *Law and Revolution: The Formation of the Western Legal Tradition*. Cambridge, Mass.: Harvard University Press, 1983.

Blankenhorn, David, Steven Bayme, and Jean Bethke Elshtain, eds. *Rebuilding the Nest: A New Commitment to the American Family*. Milwaukee: Family Service America, 1990.

Bloch, Ruth H. "Religion and Ideological Change in the American Revolution." In *Religion and American Politics: From the Colonial Period to the 1980s*, edited by Mark A. Noll, 44–61. New York: Oxford University Press, 1990.

Bratt, James D., ed. *Abraham Kuyper: A Centennial Reader.* Grand Rapids, Mich.: Eerdmans, 1998.

Carlson-Thies, Stanley W. "Charitable Choice: Bringing Religion Back into American Welfare." *Journal of Policy History* 13, no. 1 (2001), 109–132.

⏤⏤⏤, and James W. Skillen, eds. *Welfare in America: Christian Perspectives on a Policy in Crisis.* Grand Rapids, Mich.: Eerdmans, 1996.

Carr, Ann, and Mary Stewart Van Leeuwen, eds. *Religion, Feminism, and the Family.* Louisville, Ky.: Westminster John Knox Press, 1996.

Casanova, Jose. *Public Religions in the Modern World.* Chicago: University of Chicago Press, 1994.

Chaplin, Jonathan P. "Beyond Liberal Restraint: Defending Religiously Based Arguments in Law and Public Policy." *University of British Columbia Law Review* 33, no. 2 (2000).

⏤⏤⏤. "Religion and Democracy." In *Contemporary Political Studies 1998, vol. 2,* edited by Andrew Dobson and Jeffrey Stanyer, 988–1003. Political Studies Association of the United Kingdom, 1998.

⏤⏤⏤. "Subsidiarity and Sphere Sovereignty: Catholic and Reformed Conceptions of the Role of the State." In *Things Old and New: Catholic Social Teaching,* edited by Francis P. McHugh and Samuel M. Natale, 175–202. Lanham, Md.: Rowman and Littlefield, 1994.

Chubb, John, and Terry Moe. *Politics, Markets, and America's Schools.* Washington, D.C.: Brookings Institution, 1990.

Clouser, Roy A. *The Myth of Religious Neutrality.* Notre Dame, Ind.: University of Notre Dame Press, 1991.

Coleman, James, and Thomas Hoffer. *Public and Private High Schools: The Impact of Communities.* New York: Basic Books, 1987.

Conant, James B. *Thomas Jefferson and the Development of American Public Education.* Los Angeles: University of California Press, 1970.

Coons, John E., and Stephen Sugarman. *Education by Choice: The Case for Family Control.* Berkeley: University of California Press, 1978.

Crocker, David A., and Toby Linden, eds. *Ethics of Compassion: The Good Life, Justice, and Global Stewardship.* Lanham, Md.: Rowman and Littlefield, 1998.

Curry, George E., ed. *The Affirmative Action Debate.* Reading, Mass.: Addison-Wesley, 1996.

Curry-Roper, Janel, and Steven McGuire. "The Individualistic Imagination and Natural Resource Policy." *Society and Natural Resources* 6 (1993): 259–272.

Davis, David Brion. *In the Image of God: Religion, Moral Values, and Our Heritage of Slavery,* New Haven, Conn.: Yale University Press, 2001.

Dawson, Christopher. *The Gods of Revolution: An Analysis of the French Revolution.* New York: Minerva Press, 1972.

De Gruchy, John W. *Christianity and Democracy.* Cambridge: Cambridge University Press, 1995.

DeWitt, Calvin. *Caring for Creation: Responsible Stewardship of God's Handiwork.* Grand Rapids, Mich.: Baker Books, 1998.

Dionne, E. J., Jr., ed. *Community Works: The Revival of Civil Society in America.* Washington, D.C.: Brookings Institution, 1998.

———. *Why Americans Hate Politics.* New York: Simon and Schuster, 1991.

Donaldson, Dave, and Stanley Carlson-Thies. *A Revolution of Compassion: Faith-Based Groups as Full Partners in Fighting America's Social Problems.* Grand Rapids, Mich.: Baker Books, 2003.

Douglass, Frederick. *Narrative of the Life of Frederick Douglass, an American Slave.* New York: Barnes and Noble, 2002, 1845.

Drucker, Peter F. "The Age of Social Transformation." *Atlantic Monthly* (November 1994): 53–80.

Eberly, Don E., ed. *The Essential Civil Society Reader.* Lanham, Md.: Rowman and Littlefield, 2000.

Elshtain, Jean Bethke. *Power Trips and Other Journeys: Essays in Feminism as Civic Discourse.* Madison: University of Wisconsin Press, 1990.

Esbeck, Carl H. "The Establishment Clause as a Structural Restraint on Governmental Power." *Iowa Law Review* 84, no. 1 (October 1998): 1–113.

———. "Religion and the First Amendment: Some Causes of the Recent Confusion." *William and Mary Law Review* 42, no. 3 (March 2001): 907–914.

Etzioni, Amitai, ed. *New Communitarian Thinking: Persons, Virtues, Institutions, and Communities.* Charlottesville: University of Virginia Press, 1995.

Fogarty, Michael P. *Christian Democracy in Western Europe: 1820–1953.* Westport, Conn.: Greenwood Press, 1974.

Fox-Genovese, Elizabeth. *Feminism Without Illusions: A Critique of Individualism.* Chapel Hill: University of North Carolina Press, 1991.

———, et al. *Women and the Future of the Family.* Grand Rapids, Mich.: Baker Books, 2000.

Freston, Paul. *Evangelicals and Politics in Asia, Africa, and Latin America.* Cambridge: Cambridge University Press, 2001.

Galston, William A. *Liberal Pluralism: The Implications of Value Pluralism for Political Theory and Practice.* Cambridge: Cambridge University Press, 2002.

———. *Liberal Purposes: Goods, Virtues, and Diversity in the Liberal State.* New York: Cambridge University Press, 1991.

Genovese, Eugene D. *A Consuming Fire: The Fall of the Confederacy in the Mind of the White Christian South.* Athens: University of Georgia Press, 1999.

George, Robert P. *The Clash of Orthodoxies: Law, Religion, and Morality in Crisis.* Wilmington, Del.: ISI Books, 2001.

Glendon, Mary Ann. *Rights Talk: The Impoverishment of Political Discourse.* New York: Free Press, 1991.

Glenn, Charles L. *The Ambiguous Embrace: Government and Faith-Based Schools and Social Agencies.* Princeton, N.J.: Princeton University Press, 2000.

———. *The Myth of the Common School.* Amherst: University of Massachusetts Press, 1988.

Goudzwaard, Bob. *Capitalism and Progress: A Diagnosis of Western Society.* Trans. and ed. Josina Van Nuis Zylstra. Grand Rapids, Mich.: Eerdmans, 1979.

———, and Harry de Lange. *Beyond Poverty and Affluence: Toward an Economy of Care.* Trans. and ed. Mark R. Vander Vennen. Grand Rapids, Mich.: Eerdmans, 1995.

Grant, George Parkin. *Technology and Justice.* Notre Dame, Ind.: University of Notre Dame Press, 1986.

Guinier, Lani. *Lift Every Voice: Turning a Civil Rights Setback into a New Vision of Social Justice.* New York: Simon and Schuster, 1998.

Guroian, Vigen. *Ethics After Christendom: Toward an Ecclesial Christian Ethic.* Grand Rapids, Mich.: Eerdmans, 1994.

Gushee, David P., ed. *Toward a Just and Caring Society.* Grand Rapids, Mich.: Baker Books, 1999.

Gutierrez, Gustavo. *A Theology of Liberation.* Maryknoll, N.Y.: Orbis Books, 1973.

Hacker, Andrew. *Two Nations: Black and White, Separate, Hostile, Unequal.* New York: Scribners, 1992.

Hancock, Ralph C. *Calvin and the Foundations of Modern Politics.* Ithaca, N.Y.: Cornell University Press, 1989.

Healey, Robert. *Jefferson on Religion and Public Education.* New Haven, Conn.: Yale University Press, 1962.

Heslep, Robert D. *Thomas Jefferson and Education.* New York: Random House, 1969.

Hill, Steven. *Fixing Elections: The Failure of America's Winner Take All Politics.* New York: Routledge, 2002.

Hoksbergen, Roland, and Lowell M. Ewert, eds. *Local Ownership, Global Change: Will Civil Society Save the World?* Monrovia, Calif.: World Vision, 2002.

Hough, Joseph C., Jr. *Black Power and White Protestants.* New York: Oxford University Press, 1968.

Jackson, Jesse L. *Straight from the Heart.* Philadelphia: Fortress Press, 1987.

Katz, Michael. *Class, Bureaucracy, and Schools: The Illusion of Educational Change in America.* New York: Praeger, 1975.

Koch, Adrienne, and William Peden, eds. *The Life and Selected Writings of Thomas Jefferson.* New York: Modern Library, 1944.

Kolakowski, Leszek. *Modernity on Endless Trial.* Chicago: University of Chicago Press, 1990.

Koyzis, David T. *Political Visions and Illusions: A Survey and Critique of Contemporary Ideologies.* Downers Grove, Ill.: InterVarsity Press, 2003.

Kraynak, Robert P. *Christian Faith and Modern Democracy: God and Politics in the Fallen World.* Notre Dame, Ind.: University of Notre Dame Press, 2001.

Kselman, Thomas, and Joseph A. Buttigieg, eds. *European Christian Democracy: Historical Legacies and Comparative Perspectives.* Notre Dame, Ind.: University of Notre Dame Press, 2003.

Kuyper, Abraham. *The Problem of Poverty*. Edited by James W. Skillen. Grand Rapids, Mich.: Baker Book House, 1991.

Lasch, Christopher. *The True and Only Heaven: Progress and Its Critics*. New York: W.W. Norton, 1991.

Lemann, Nicholas. *The Promised Land: The Great Black Migration and How It Changed America*. New York: Knopf, 1991.

Lieberman, Myron. *Privatization and Educational Choice*. New York: St. Martin's Press, 1989.

Lijphart, Arend, and Bernard Grofman, eds. *Choosing an Electoral System: Issues and Alternatives*. New York: Praeger, 1984.

Lind, Michael. "A Radical Plan to Change American Politics." *Atlantic Monthly* (August 1992): 73–83.

Locke, John. *Two Treatises of Government*. Edited by Thomas I. Cook. New York: Hafner Press, 1973.

Loury, Glenn C. "Affirmative Action: Is It Just?" In *The Constitutional Bases of Political and Social Change in the United States*, edited by Schlomo Slonimn, 109–139. New York: Praeger, 1990.

———. *One by One, From the Inside Out: Essays and Reviews on Race and Responsibility in America*. New York: Free Press, 1995.

Lowi, Theodore J. *The End of Liberalism: The Second Republic of the United States*. New York: W. W. Norton, 1979.

Lutz, Donald S. *The Origins of American Constitutionalism*. Baton Rouge: Louisiana State University Press, 1988.

MacIntyre, Alasdair. *After Virtue: A Study in Moral Theory*. Notre Dame, Ind.: University of Notre Dame Press, 1981.

Maier, Hans. *Revolution and Church: The Early History of Christian Democracy: 1789–1901*. Trans. Emily M. Schossberger. Notre Dame, Ind.: University of Notre Dame Press, 1969.

Manis, Andrew Michael. *Southern Civil Religions in Conflict: Black and White Baptists and Civil Rights, 1847–1957*. Athens: University of Georgia Press, 1987.

Marshall, Paul. *God and the Constitution: Christianity and American Politics*. Lanham, Md.: Rowman and Littlefield, 2002.

———. "Two Types of Rights." *Canadian Journal of Political Science* 25, no. 4 (1992): 661–676.

McCarthy, Rockne, James W. Skillen, and William A. Harper. *Disestablishment a Second Time: Genuine Pluralism for American Schools*. Grand Rapids, Mich.: Eerdmans, 1982.

McCarthy, Rockne, et al. *Society, State, and Schools: A Case for Structural and Confessional Pluralism*. Grand Rapids, Mich.: Eerdmans, 1981.

Mead, Lawrence M. *Beyond Entitlement: The Social Obligations of Citizenship*. New York: Free Press, 1986.

Miguez Bonino, Jose. *Toward a Christian Political Ethics*. Philadelphia: Fortress Press, 1983.

Miller, John C., ed. *Curing World Poverty: The New Role of Property*. St. Louis: Social Justice Review, 1994.

Monsma, Stephen V. *Positive Neutrality*. Westport, Conn.: Greenwood Press, 1993.

———. "Substantive Neutrality as a Basis for Free Exercise–No Establishment Common Ground." *Journal of Church and State* 42 (Winter 2000): 13–35.

———, and J. Christopher Soper, eds. *Equal Treatment of Religion in a Pluralistic Society*. Grand Rapids, Mich.: Eerdmans, 1998.

Nelson, Robert N. *Economics as Religion: From Samuelson to Chicago and Beyond*. University Park, Pa.: Penn State University Press, 2001.

Neuhaus, Richard John, ed. *Democracy and the Renewal of Public Education*. Grand Rapids, Mich.: Eerdmans, 1987.

———. *The Naked Public Square: Religion and Democracy in America*. Grand Rapids, Mich.: Eerdmans, 1984.

Noll, Mark A. *America's God: From Jonathan Edwards to Abraham Lincoln*. New York: Oxford University Press, 2002.

Novak, David. *Jewish Social Ethics*. New York: Oxford University Press, 1992.

Oates, Stephen B. *Let the Trumpet Sound: The Life of Martin Luther King, Jr.* New York: New American Library, 1982.

O'Connell, Brian. *Civil Society: The Underpinnings of American Democracy*. Hanover, N.H.: University Press of New England, 1999.

O'Donovan, Oliver. *The Desire of the Nations: Rediscovering the Roots of Political Theology*. Cambridge: Cambridge University Press, 1996.

Owen, J. Judd. *Religion and the Demise of Liberal Rationalism*. Chicago: University of Chicago Press, 2001.

Pangle, Thomas L. *Political Philosophy and the God of Abraham*. Baltimore: Johns Hopkins University Press, 2003.

Papini, Roberto. *Christian Democrat International*. Trans. Robert Royal. Lanham, Md.: Rowman and Littlefield, 1996.

Patterson, James T. *Brown v. Board of Education: A Civil Rights Milestone and Its Troubled Legacy*. New York: Oxford University Press, 2001.

Percy, Walker. *Walker Percy: Sign-Posts in a Strange Land*. Edited by Patrick Samway. New York: Noonday Press, 1991.

Putnam, Robert. *Bowling Alone: The Collapse and Revival of American Community*. New York: Simon and Schuster, 2000.

Ravitch, Diane. *The Great School Wars: New York City, 1805–1973*. New York: Basic Books, 1974.

Reichley, A. James, ed. *Elections American Style*. Washington, D.C.: Brookings Institution, 1987.

Richey, Russell E., and Donald C. Jones. *American Civil Religion*. New York: Harper Forum Books, 1974.

Rosenberg, Gerard N. *The Hollow Hope*. Chicago: University of Chicago Press, 1991.

Rudolph, Frederick, ed. *Essays on Education in the Early Republic*. Cambridge, Mass.: Harvard University Press, 1965.

Sandel, Michael J. *Democracy's Discontent: America in Search of a Public Philosophy.* Cambridge, Mass.: Harvard University Belknap Press, 1996.

———. *Liberalism and the Limits of Justice.* Cambridge: Cambridge University Press, 1982.

Seligman, Adam. *The Idea of Civil Society.* Princeton, N.J.: Princeton University Press, 1992.

Sen, Amartya. *Development as Freedom.* New York: Anchor Books, 1999.

Sigmund, Paul E. *Liberation Theology at the Crossroads: Democracy or Revolution?* New York: Oxford University Press, 1990.

Singley, Bernestine, ed. *When Race Becomes Real: Black and White Writers Confront Their Personal Histories.* Chicago: Lawrence Hill Books, 2002.

Skillen, James W. "Going Beyond Liberalism to Christian Social Philosophy." *Christian Scholar's Review* 19, no. 3 (March 1990): 220–230.

———. *Recharging the American Experiment: Principled Pluralism for Genuine Civic Community.* Grand Rapids, Mich.: Baker Books, 1994.

———. *The Scattered Voice: Christians at Odds in the Public Square.* Grand Rapids, Mich.: Zondervan, 1990.

———, ed. *The School Choice-Controversy: What Is Constitutional?* Grand Rapids, Mich.: Baker Books, 1993.

———, and Rockne M. McCarthy, eds. *Political Order and the Plural Structure of Society.* Atlanta: Scholar's Press, 1991.

Steele, Shelby. *The Content of Our Character.* New York: St. Martin's Press, 1990.

Stevenson, William R., Jr. *Sovereign Grace: The Place and Significance of Christian Freedom in John Calvin's Political Thought.* New York: Oxford University Press, 1999.

Stiltner, Brian. "Reassessing Religion's Place in a Liberal Democracy." *Religious Studies Review* (October 2000): 319–325.

Strauss, Leo. *Natural Right and History.* Chicago: University of Chicago Press, 1953.

Sundquist, James L. *Constitutional Reform and Effective Government.* Rev. ed. Washington, D.C.: Brookings Institution, 1992.

Teixeira, Ruy A. *The Disappearing American Voter.* Washington, D.C.: Brookings Institution, 1992.

Thiemann, Ronald F. *Religion in Public Life: A Dilemma for Democracy.* Washington, D.C.: Georgetown University Press, 1996.

Tinder, Glenn. *The Political Meaning of Christianity: An Interpretation.* Baton Rouge: Louisiana State University Press, 1989.

Tyack, David B., ed. *Turning Points in American Educational History.* Lexington, Mass.: Xerox College Publishing, 1967.

Van Creveld, Martin. *The Rise and Decline of the State.* Cambridge: Cambridge University Press, 1999.

Van Dyke, Harry. *Groen van Prinsterer's Lectures on Unbelief and Revolution.* Jordan Station, Ontario: Wedge Publishing Foundation, 1989.

Van Leeuwen, Mary Stewart, ed. *After Eden: Facing the Challenge of Gender Reconciliation.* Grand Rapids, Mich.: Eerdmans, 1993.

Voegelin, Eric. *From Enlightenment to Revolution.* Edited by John H. Hallowell. Durham, N.C.: Duke University Press, 1975.

———. *The New Science of Politics.* Chicago: University of Chicago Press, 1952.

Walzer, Michael. "A Community of Communities." In *Debating Democracy's Discontent: Essays on American Politics, Law and Public Philosophy,* edited by Anita L. Allen and Milton C. Regan. New York: Oxford University Press, 1998.

———. *Spheres of Justice: A Defense of Pluralism and Equality.* New York: Basic Books, 1983.

Wattenberg, Martin P. *The Rise of Candidate-Centered Politics.* Cambridge, Mass.: Harvard University Press, 1991.

Will, George F. *Restoration: Congress, Term Limits and the Recovery of Deliberative Democracy.* New York: Free Press, 1992.

Witte, John, Jr. *Religion and the American Constitutional Experiment: Essential Rights and Liberties.* Boulder, Colo.: Westview Press, 2000.

———, ed. *Christianity and Democracy in Global Context.* Boulder, Colo.: Westview Press, 1993.

———, and Johan van der Vyver, eds. *Religious Human Rights in Global Perspective: Religious Perspectives.* The Hague: Martinus Nijhoff Publishers, 1996.

Wolfe, Alan. *Whose Keepers? Social Science and Moral Obligation.* Berkeley: University of California Press, 1989.

Wolterstorff, Nicholas, and Robert Audi. *Religion in the Public Square: The Place of Religious Convictions in Political Debate.* Lanham, Md.: Rowman and Littlefield, 1997.

Zagorin, Perez. *How the Idea of Religious Toleration Came to the West.* Princeton, N.J.: Princeton University Press, 2003.

Index

ACLU. *See* American Civil Liberties Union

Adams, John, 97

America/American, 4–8, 19, 24, 26–27; Civil War, 5–6, 77, 81, 83–84, 123–24, 130; colonial period, 4, 60–61; exceptionalism, 6, 61; republic, 4, 59–63, 67, 89–90, 92, 95–97, 102–3, 106, 124, 127, 129–33; Revolution, 4

American Civil Liberties Union (ACLU), 63

Americans United for the Separation of Church and State, 63, 67, 72

Audi, Robert, 156n13

Augustine, Saint, 55

Barber, Benjamin, 19, 21

Bennett, W. Lance, 133, 135–37, 164n12, 164n14, 165n17

Bohman, James, 66

Catholic Charities, 65, 74, 155n12

Catholic social thought, 9, 149n12

chaplaincy, military, 70–72

Charitable Choice. *See* welfare

Chesterton, G. K., 61, 85

Christian Coalition, 66–67, 69

Christian-democratic: parties, 5–6; perspective, 2–17, 31–32, 57–58, 73, 86, 88–90, 92, 109, 127, 131–32, 146

Chubb, John, 93, 102

citizenship, 4, 27, 35, 48, 83, 95–96, 100, 105–6, 129–46

civil religion, 5, 61–62, 64, 66, 82, 85–86, 90

civil rights, 6, 10–11, 78, 80, 82–87, 89–90; equal treatment, 2–3, 11–13, 60, 69, 77–78, 88–90, 101, 109, 125; religious freedom, 5, 9, 11, 60, 62, 64–67, 73, 84, 86, 92, 94, 101–3, 107–9; voting rights, 4, 129–46

civil society/mediating structures, 20–40, 117, 120–21, 131, 149n3, 150n13, 150n26, 150n27. *See also* pluralism

Clark, Justice Thomas, 100–101

Cleaver, Eldridge, 157n2

commons/commonwealth, 115, 117–21, 123, 127

About the Author

James W. Skillen is president of the Center for Public Justice, which he has directed since 1981, and is the editor of its *Public Justice Report* (quarterly) and *Capital Commentary* (bi-monthly). He earned his B.A. in philosophy at Wheaton College, the B.D. at Westminster Theological Seminary, and the M.A. and Ph.D. in political science at Duke University.

He is the author or editor of sixteen books, including *A Covenant to Keep: Meditations on the Biblical Theme of Justice* (2000); *Recharging the American Experiment: Principled Pluralism for Genuine Civic Community* (1994); *The Scattered Voice: Christians at Odds in the Public Square* (1990); and, as coeditor, *Welfare in America: Christian Perspectives on a Policy in Crisis* (with Stanley Carlson-Thies, 1996), and *Political Order and the Plural Structure of Society* (with Rockne McCarthy, 1991).

A frequent speaker in civic forums and on college campuses, Skillen has lectured on Christian-democratic themes at conferences and universities in Canada, Europe, Russia, Korea, and South Africa. He and Doreen, the parents of Jeanene and Jamie, live in Annapolis, Maryland.